The Real
Woodrow Wilson

Portions of the Introduction appeared in somewhat different form in the *Philadelphia Inquirer*.

1 2 3 4 5 6 7 8 9 10 XXX 08 07 06 05 04 03 02 01

Library of Congress Cataloging-in-Publication Data

Link, Arthur Stanley.
    The real Woodrow Wilson : an interview with Arthur S. Link,
    editor of the Wilson papers / by James Robert Carroll.— 1st ed.
        p.   cm.
    Includes bibliographical references.
    ISBN 1-884592-32-5
        1. Wilson, Woodrow, 1856-1924.   2. Presidents—United
States—Biography.   3. Link, Arthur Stanley—Interviews.   4.
Historians—United States—Interviews.   I. Carroll, James Robert,
1951-   II. Title.
E767 .L645   2001
973.91'3'092—dc21

                                                            00-011424

Copyright © 2001 James Robert Carroll
Published by Images from the Past, Inc.
P.O. Box 137, Bennington VT 05201
http://www.ImagesfromthePast.com

Printed in the United States of America

Design and Production: Stillwater Studio, Stillwater, NY
Printer: Thomson-Shore, Inc., Dexter, MI
Text: Palatino 10/14; *Display:* Mona Lisa Solid
Paper: 55# Writers Offset B21 Natural

The Real
Woodrow Wilson

An Interview with Arthur S. Link,
Editor of the Wilson Papers

By James Robert Carroll

Images from the Past
Bennington, Vermont

For my dear wife, Carol

My collaborator in life

CONTENTS

ACKNOWLEDGMENTS

This has been a project whose genesis was more than seven years ago. But unlike at the Academy Awards, the red light isn't blinking and the director isn't giving me the "wind it up" sign as the orchestra swells. Here I wish to give unhurried acknowledgement of my debt to the many people who did things great and small to bring *The Real Woodrow Wilson* to reality.

Not a jot of this work could have happened without the kind indulgence of the late Arthur S. Link, a gentleman's gentleman. He gave me all the time I needed – and then some – and answered numerous follow-up inquiries later. In Link's hands and, as you will see, in his words, even the most uninterested person on earth would have been unable to resist the Wilson story. No proper thanks seems sufficient. I consider this entire project an appreciation for Link's gift to scholarship, to the American people, and to the world.

Next on my list are the imaginative journalists at the *Philadelphia Inquirer* Sunday magazine who took a chance on a speculative story idea about a scholar finishing his life's work: Avery Rome and Michael Mills. If they hadn't said "yes" to a piece on Link, you wouldn't be reading this now.

At the *Courier-Journal* in Louisville, I greatly appreciate the encouragement and understanding of Bennie L. Ivory, Arthur B. Post, Jr., John A. Mura, Debi Yetter, Al Cross, James Malone, and, most especially, Gideon Gil, fellow Boston Red Sox sufferer. Without their flexibility at a few crucial moments, completion of this work would have been impossible.

Appreciation also goes to many in the Gannett News Service Washington Bureau, and particularly to John Hanchette, who is wise and witty.

For my early work on Link, I am grateful to some current and former editors at the *Press-Telegram* in Long Beach, California, for freeing me up from my usual Washington reporting duties: James Crutchfield, Rich Archbold, John Futch, James Robinson, Bill Hillburg, with extra nods to Michael Schwartz and Andy Alderette.

In the Knight-Ridder Newspapers Washington Bureau, I owe thanks as well to a battalion of colleagues, some still there and others who have moved on, who provided guidance and support in many ways. A special tip of the cap to Tom Farragher, now at the *Boston Globe*, for his unfailing friendship, unfiltered perspective, and devilish antics. And my heartfelt thanks to Steven Thomma in the Knight-Ridder bureau, a pal who has been good counsel and great company, and who likes to talk about presidential history almost as much as I do.

Historians Arthur M. Schlesinger, Jr., and August Heckscher gave me very useful perspectives on Link's work, and George S. McGovern, former presidential candidate and former senator from South Dakota, was kind enough to share his impressions of his thesis advisor.

I also wish to thank Link's daughter, Peggy Link Weil, and one of his sons, William Link, for pulling pictures of their father from the family archives.

This book wouldn't be what it is without the hours of time generously given to me by Frank J. Aucella, museum director of the Woodrow Wilson House in Washington. He was a tremendous resource for historical information, and he kindly opened up the picture archives to share what you see within these pages. And it was his suggestion that led me to my publisher, about which more below. I also want to thank the Wilson House's curator, Margaret M. Nowack, for guidance through the files. I also am happy to have had the aid of Rick Potter, curator at the Woodrow Wilson Birthplace in Staunton, Virginia, who shared the photographic treasures in his care.

Some of the additional photography in this book is the handiwork of Bill Perry in the Gannett News Service Washington Bureau. He knows his craft, as you can see.

Conceptualizing the look of a book, from jacket design to type size, is one of those mysterious processes made a little more accessible by this work's designer,

Susan Mathews. I have only unending awe for her efforts and the stunning results.

Sarah Novak is precisely the editor every writer needs: she was gentle on the prose, but ferocious on precision and clarity. Every suggestion she made improved this work.

My publisher, Tordis Ilg Isselhardt, is a secret I would prefer best kept to very few. If the world's writers discover her, she will never have a moment's peace. She took a flyer on a total stranger, exuded absolute enthusiasm for this project from start to finish, made *everything* painless, has an intimate familiarity with all aspects of the precarious business of book publishing, and absolutely loves her work. There is not enough I can say to express my profound gratitude. I forgot to mention the fun. This was a magnificent adventure.

Many thanks, too, to Collins Sennett at Images from the Past for her cheer and help.

I am blessed with a very close family, and I want to acknowledge the immeasurable contributions to this project – in love, intellectual stimulation, kibitzing, banter, and horseplay – by my sister, Nancy E. Carroll, my brothers, Peter G. Carroll and Sean B. Carroll, my mother and fellow presidential enthusiast, Joan Hebert Carroll, and to my late father, Joseph Robert Carroll, who sparked the love of inquiry in me at a very early age, and from whom I inherited a passion for books.

Finally, to my wife, Carol Vernon, I owe all that is humanly possible to express. She endured the inevitable interruptions to family routine not just with graceful tolerance, but with humor. She covered the details and took on whatever was necessary to help in the birth of this work. Carol has been my rabid backer, my first reader, (helpful) critic and editor, and my loving partner in every way on this book, which also is dedicated to her.

Wait – now this is really "finally," and I can hear that orchestra swelling – I have to thank my daughters, Fiona, six, and Brenna, five, for being incredibly patient with their father. At one point, they insisted on joining me on a trip for this book, a forty-eight-hour, 1,000-mile roundtrip car ride between Virginia and New England. They, and their mother, were troopers, dream companions on this odyssey.

James R. Carroll
Alexandria, Virginia
July 14, 2000

INTRODUCTION

In February 2000, on Presidents Day, the C-SPAN cable television network released a survey of fifty-eight presidential historians, biographers, and observers of the Oval Office as part of its year-long series *American Presidents: Life Portraits.* The survey assessed the forty-one men who have served as the nation's chief executive. Those surveyed were asked to measure each president based on ten qualities of presidential leadership: persuading the public, leading in a crisis, managing the economy, being a moral authority for the country, handling international relations, showing administrative skills, dealing with Congress, having a vision and setting an agenda, pursuing equal justice for all, and performing within the context of the times.

The first four presidents at the top of the list were the same ones who have topped many other such surveys over recent decades: Abraham Lincoln, Franklin D. Roosevelt, George Washington, and Theodore Roosevelt. At number five, his stock still rising steadily, was Harry S. Truman. And then, placing sixth, ahead of Thomas Jefferson, John F. Kennedy, Dwight D. Eisenhower, and Lyndon B. Johnson, was Woodrow Wilson, the nation's twenty-eighth president.

Among these ten great leaders, Wilson without question is the least known to most Americans at the opening of the twenty-first century. There are many possible explanations for this. Wilson as a personality has seemed rather inaccessible, lacking in dynamism. Indeed, at first glance he looks somewhat colorless up against his competition at the head of the pack. His life story also appears to lack drama – again, especially in comparison with other top presidents. Then, too, World War I, the central crisis of Wilson's presidency, has not excited the imaginations of recent generations as much as the struggle for independence, the Civil War, and World War II.

Yet these public perceptions of Wilson miss the mark. Fortunately, one needn't look far to get a sense of the real Wilson. And we can credit that to one man more than any other: historian Arthur Stanley Link.

This book consists of an extended conversation I had with Link on July 18, 1993, as his Herculean task as editor of *The Papers of Woodrow Wilson* was coming to a close after some thirty-five years. This was one of the happy opportunities I have had from time to time in my career to combine my passion for American history and presidential politics with my chosen profession as a journalist. I had come to Link's leafy summer place in Montreat, North Carolina, to interview him for a story about the Wilson papers that later appeared in the *Philadelphia Inquirer* Sunday magazine.

In the years since that memorable afternoon, I often thought about how that interview brought Woodrow Wilson alive. Not incidentally, it captured Arthur Link out from behind his duties, excited all over again as he relived the full-throated chase of his elusive and complex quarry. Here, truly, were history and historian in joyous struggle. The purpose of this book is, simply, to share some of this magic. I hope this modest effort will help serve in the cause of a better understanding of Wilson, and acquaint the general reader, as well as the scholar, with Link's singular achievement.

Hence, the somewhat unusual format of a conversation. I wanted to preserve the flavor, the spontaneity, and the surprise of a well-told tale of the story behind the story. This, however, is not an original idea. We see this in the published proceedings of conferences. The closest model to this book, however, is *Malone & Jefferson: The Biographer and the Sage,* an interview with Dumas Malone, the preeminent biographer of Thomas Jefferson, published by the University of Virginia Library in 1981.

One additional word about format. I have divided up the conversation into subject areas. But as is usual in any lengthy give-and-take, tangents and irrelevancies intrude. Those have been excised. So, too, the order of topics can become jumbled. Throughout this interview, Link and I returned to some topics a couple of times. For purposes of clarity and organization, some segments of the conversation have been reordered. I have added words here and there to clarify or complete a comment and I have added fuller names and other identifying information where needed. These additions are shown in brackets. Also, ellipsis points have been placed where there have been deletions. They also have been used where a speaker paused or was interrupted.

This is, by no means, a complete survey of Wilson's life and presidency, but rather an overview of important points about the man and his work, told in the context of his papers by the historian who knew him best. We do not cover, just to name a couple of events, Wilson's military interventions in Mexico and Russia, nor his appointment of Louis Brandeis to the United States Supreme Court – the first Jewish jurist to be chosen for the high court. I hope, however, that this work will encourage readers to dip into some of the books listed in the bibliography.

I also have added a chronology of Wilson's life to provide the reader with some helpful guideposts along the way.

As the reader will see, Link made Woodrow Wilson his life's work. It began as a Ph.D dissertation, then grew into a book in 1947 titled *Wilson: The Road to the White House*. The work traces Wilson from his days in academia to his maverick entrance into politics as governor of New Jersey. That first book led to four more – two of which won the Bancroft Prize in History – that chronicled

Wilson's presidency up to the nation's entry into World War I. Link figured there would have been at least four more books, taking Wilson through the war, to the arduous negotiations over the Versailles Treaty, then into the grueling campaign for the League of Nations that led to the strokes that disabled him and his presidency. Link wrote about a hundred articles and many other books on various aspects of Wilson's time in the White House, but those other four books to complete the Wilson biography were never written.

Instead, by the early 1960s, Link's energies increasingly were devoted to being editor of the papers of Woodrow Wilson, a project for which he was picked by a committee of fellow historians. In a way, this was the ultimate biography, the story of a life told entirely through primary sources – mountains of them.

In the fall of 1963, Link and his band of researchers and editors already had been working on the Wilson papers for four years. In a scholarly equivalent of a shopvac, the Link operation had scooped up paper, box by box, piece by piece, sometimes scrap by scrap. The team had hunted from Alabama to Argentina, from Canada to England to France, from the Ford Motor Company to the Wilmington, North Carolina, Public Library, cajoling universities, libraries, archives, the prominent and the unknown to part with prized letters and documents long enough to get them to a copying machine.

The job appeared nearly done. Then came the phone call from the Woodrow Wilson House in Washington about an amazing discovery: thousands upon thousands of papers in steel steamer trunks documenting the hitherto sketchy early life of the future president. It was as if the papers had been waiting for the right caretaker, the one person who could make sense of their story. Peering breathlessly back at them was, indeed, the right man.

They were born about fifty miles and sixty-four years apart.

Thomas Woodrow Wilson, the son of a minister, was born in 1856 in Staunton, Virginia, in the Shenandoah Valley. Arthur S. Link, also the son of a minister, was born in 1920 in Newmarket, Virginia, also in the Shenandoah Valley. Wilson lived in the South as a youth – including in South Carolina and North Carolina – ultimately became a scholar and rose to prominence at Princeton University as its president, and went into politics as a Democrat. Link, too, spent his youth in the South – in North Carolina – graduated from the University of North Carolina, went on to get his doctorate from there, but likewise came to prominence at Princeton. Link, too, had a passion for politics, at one point writing speeches for Democratic presidential candidate (and former Link student) George McGovern.

At the time of his encounter with the steamer trunks, Link had Volume 1 of *The Papers of Woodrow Wilson* being readied for publication. It was put aside. Then, finally, three years after those wondrous trunks were dragged from the darkness, the real Volume 1 appeared from Princeton University Press. It was followed by Volume 2 ... Volume 3 ... Volume 20 ... Volume 40 ... and, in 1994, the final installment: a closing essay and final index that was Volume 69. Funded by the Woodrow Wilson Foundation with considerable support in facilities and staff from Princeton, the Wilson project not only is the most comprehensive collection of writings and documents ever assembled for Woodrow Wilson, but also is the most massive such work on any president or American historical figure.

Here, Wilson is open to the world to meet, to probe, to analyze, as much as a published record of a man's life can possibly allow.

By Link's estimate, he assembled about a quarter of a million documents running in their original length between 500,000 and 600,000 pages. In those pages are many papers never previously made public. Some were even secret. These gems shed new light on events in the first part of the twentieth century, as well as on Wilson's life. Peeling away historical guesswork and suppositions about Wilson's inner self, the papers revealed, among other things, startling and critical new facts about a president who was far sicker and debilitated at the end of his term than anyone had imagined.

Historian Arthur Schlesinger, Jr., was on the committee of scholars that tapped Link as the Wilson papers editor in 1958. The choice, Schlesinger told me as the papers were nearing the last volume, "was self-evident." The results, he said, are "an extraordinary accomplishment … a landmark in historical scholarship."

Extraordinary indeed. The papers are not, as some might presume, just dull governmental stuff strictly for academics. Beginning with the first entry of his birth in the family Bible in 1856 and running through to the last days of Wilson's life in 1924, the papers are rich in details of daily living, revealing in their depiction of Wilson, his family and friends and their personal lives.

Thankfully, Wilson and his family were great savers of the handwritten and typewritten word. Consider this endearing moment of self-doubt from Wilson at the tender age of nineteen, from his shorthand diary:

> *(October) 27th Friday (1876) … I have come to the conclusion that my friends have no doubt come to long ago and that is my mind is a very ordinary one indeed. I am nothing as far as intellect goes. But I can plod and work….*

Of course, to Link and other historians, this is supremely amusing, coming from a man who would be known for his intellect and scholarship long before he ever entered politics.

The reader of *The Papers of Woodrow Wilson* discovers a man who is a baseball fanatic, a singer, a reciter and sometimes composer of limericks, a prankster, a mimic who could wiggle his ears and nose and dislocate his jaw for comic effect. Perhaps most revealing, Wilson was a proficient love-letter writer to his first wife, Ellen Louise Axson Wilson, who died of kidney disease in 1914, and to his second wife, Edith Bolling Galt Wilson. Link tells the fascinating story of how he found these priceless intimacies, once thought to be lost, and saved other batches from the incinerator.

Here is a sample missive from Wilson to his future first wife, Ellen:

> *Balto., Sabbath afternoon*
> *Jany. 25, 1885*

My own darling,

> *... Why do I delight so, I wonder, in telling you of my love for you over and over again, my little sweetheart? You know that I love you – and, even if you don't know how much, there's no use trying to tell you that – because I've tried often enough to know that I can't....*

*If love can make a true husband, I will be one to
my darling, my matchless little queen ... whom I
love more and more as the day of our marriage
approaches, and whom then I shall serve as*

*Her own
Woodrow*

And, despite his Victorian times, Wilson also could
be surprisingly frank about sex. Again, to Ellen:

Balto., May 31, 1885

My own darling,

*... You did not tell me till just the other day,
precious, that you are fond of being petted .... Ah,
my little queen, you don't know what a precious
privilege it is in my eyes to be free to use every
language of love to you. If you love to be petted, you
are going to marry some one who dearly loves to pet
you. His past conduct must have already satisfied
you on that point!*

... Keep for yourself as much love as you can
dream of in a score of day-dreams about such love as
you want from

Your own
Woodrow

Needless to say, this is a side of Woodrow Wilson different from what all but a few close associates – perhaps not even them – ever knew.

Link got to know Edith Wilson – that's how he came to salvage her love letters. But equally important, he had that wonderful chance a historian treasures to evaluate in person one of the participants in great events. Active in humanitarian causes and historic preservation (including Wilson's birthplace and the S Street house), Edith Wilson never quite dispelled the image of her as "Madame President" at the end of her husband's second term in the White House. Link tells how, except in two cases, Mrs. Wilson really had no interest in wielding power.

Link's most significant revelations relate to Wilson's declining health as he struggled to win Senate ratification of the Treaty of Versailles. The historical sleuthing in pursuit of clues about Wilson's medical condition at various times in his life produced rewards beyond imagining, doing nothing less than changing how future historians and biographers – and readers – perceive the twenty-eighth president. While not as visible as Franklin D. Roosevelt's battle with polio, Wilson's lifelong affliction with hypertension, the resulting strokes – including at least two before he became president – and an undercurrent of increasing fragility make for a compelling personal drama in its own right. As illness overwhelmed Wilson, the hope that the "Great War" was the "war to end all wars" faded – although few could see that so clearly at the time.

Silver-haired and approaching his seventy-third birthday at the time of our conversation, Link sat for hours talking about Wilson. At first, I felt somewhat intimidated by the idea of interviewing this American historian of the first rank. After all, I hadn't read the sixty-eight volumes of the Wilson Papers already published. Link couldn't have been more gracious, and put me at ease immediately. There was an element of curiosity, on his part, why anyone beyond the world of fellow scholars would be interested in what he had to say, in the story he had to tell. But he also was proud of what he had accomplished. At one point, his eyes filled with tears as he talked about the end of his project at Volume 69.

Link never tired of his subject, Woodrow Wilson. He quoted from speeches and letters and memorandums, sometimes verbatim, referred to dates and people, all without a single note. As we sat in a comfortable, wood-paneled room, with rain cascading through the trees outside – at one point, we talked through a crashing thunderstorm – not one volume of the Wilson Papers was at hand. It is as if Link had lived the era himself. Indeed, it is not much of an exaggeration to say that to sit down with Arthur Link was the closest thing to meeting our twenty-eighth president. Please join us.

Arthur S. Link, behind Wilson's desk at Princeton, in the 1960s.

"LITTLE DID THEY KNOW:"
The Beginnings of the
Wilson Papers Project

CARROLL: How did you get interested in Wilson originally?

LINK: I really wasn't interested in Wilson primarily. I was trained as a Southern historian at Chapel Hill, interested in twentieth century history – this would be the late '30s, early '40s. And, of course, there wasn't much written about it.

My main interest at the time was the progressive movement in the South. In fact, if I may say so, I think I discovered it. Quite a very lively movement. Hardly different at all from Wisconsin and the Middle West. So I was searching about for a dissertation topic – this was '41, '42, I was at the University of North Carolina – and just at that moment the Wilson papers were opened to researchers. I think I was the second person to use them after Mr. [Ray Stannard] Baker, the official biographer, had finished. So I got terribly interested in the Democratic campaign of 1910 to 12. The Democratic

Party was very much like today, transforming itself from an agrarian, populist party … pretty much a bourbon-populist party, with conflicting traditions. [William Jennings] Bryan had announced in 1910 that he wasn't going to run for president in 1912 …

CARROLL: At long last.

LINK: At long last, exactly – after three tries. So this opened the field. And Wilson comes out, the governor of New Jersey. There really wasn't much on Wilson. We have Baker and we have [Joseph] Tumulty and the memoirs and things like that. But what fascinated me was, here's a man who is, I thought slightly mistakenly, who had been a pure academic. He'd been in academic affairs all his life, except for a brief, one-year try at law. Suddenly [he was] going as it were from the presidency of a small university [Princeton] to the presidency of the United States. How in the world could this happen?

I did my dissertation on the South and the Democratic campaign of 1910 to 12. This involved vast newspaper researches and as much manuscript research as one could do in those days, which wasn't a great deal. And I saw in the South a lively two-party system – and a tremendous amount of support for Wilson. And that's really how I first got intrigued by this man.

THE REAL WOODROW WILSON

I went to Columbia University in 1944-45. I was in Henry Steele Commager's seminar. And Commager was very interested in this subject. And I said I'd like to start a book on the political education of Woodrow Wilson. Which is what I did. I really started about 1909-1910, [Wilson's] entry into politics in New Jersey.

CARROLL: You were doing what at that time?

LINK: I did my doctoral work entirely backwards. I graduated with my [bachelor's degree] in 1941. I tried to get into the Navy and Air Force, but I couldn't do it. I thought I was going to be drafted. So I said, why don't I – by that time I knew what I wanted to write my dissertation on – at least get started on the dissertation. Then I got, not deferred, I got turned down. So I went ahead and wrote my Ph.D dissertation without taking any courses beyond the [master's degree], without taking my general examinations. One year, '43 or '44, I taught in the Army program at North Carolina State in Raleigh. That's when I studied for my generals, passed my generals, in 1944. I was ready to take my Ph.D, and they said: "But you haven't got enough course credits." So they said: "Why don't you go up to Columbia – you've been here five, six years and you got everything we have to give you – and go up for a year and take some courses and do your own work?" Which is what I did. In Commager's seminar I started this book. I did an enormous amount of newspaper research, particularly the coverage of the New Jersey period, the governorship, as well as the presidential campaign.

CARROLL: In those days, nothing was on microfiche?

LINK: Oh no, gracious me. I went through 325 newspapers for a two-year period. Just knocking it out on my typewriter. We didn't have Xerox back in those days. I was working twelve, fourteen hours a day in what we used to call the Annex of the Library of Congress, I think it's now called the Jefferson Building, right across the street from the old building. Anyhow, I finished this book.

Meanwhile, we had just moved to Princeton, in 1945, because I was appointed an instructor. I took my manuscript down to the then-director of the Princeton [University] Press, Davis Smith, Jr. He read it and was terribly excited and he said, "Look, Arthur, you've got the makings here of a wonderful first volume in a two-volume biography of Wilson. Why don't you add some chapters?" I had started some chapters covering his early life. "You could go through, as you do, the election of 1912, and then you could complete his life in one more volume." I said, "Fine, I'll be back." And I did. And that's how *Wilson: The Road to the White House* came out. So that was 1947.

CARROLL: Little did you know.

LINK: Little did I know. But I must say by that time I was really hooked on Wilson.

CARROLL: What intrigued you about Wilson: he was not as well known as people thought? Were you being surprised by him all the time?

LINK: It's hard to say what intrigued me most. So many things did intrigue me. Now mind you, I didn't know all that much about Wilson at this time. But I knew enough to realize I was dealing with a really first-class individual, a person of just unbelievable abilities, an obvious genius. A man of enormous oratorical ability, a marvelous writer, a great scholar. I guess there was a personal element, too. We were born about forty miles apart. I was born in Newmarket, Virginia. He was born in Staunton, Virginia, of course. We both came from similar backgrounds, ministerial backgrounds. My father was a minister. Wilson's father was a minister …. I think Wilson's integrity, his courage, and above all his extraordinary political skills intrigued me. As I say, at this point, I didn't know all that much about him, but I knew enough to think, "Well, here's a person really worth putting a lot of time into."

CARROLL: Did Ray Stannard Baker's eight-volume biography of Wilson [published from 1927 to 1939] seem kind of intimidating to you? I guess you were trying to bring something new to Wilson.

LINK: Yes. As you know, Baker's pretty much is a personal biography, not very deep in political or diplomatic history. I think it's a marvelous biography, the type that it is. But I'm primarily a historical biographer, really a historian. Baker was primarily a … well, a journalist, if you'll pardon me. It was a journalistic type of biography. At that time, I really didn't have that much interest in Wilson personally. I was interested more in how he fit in in the context and history of the time. All that changed as I got to know him better and better. And I think *The Road to the White House*, once you get into the New Jersey politics, is a pretty good book. But I'm sure I would write it differently if I were …

CARROLL: Really?

LINK: … Oh indeed, I certainly would. I've got one excuse. When I started the work, the papers, the essential papers, of his early life, simply were not available. First of all, the correspondence between Wilson and his first wife were closed. Secondly, the correspondence with his lady friend, Mrs. Mary Ann Hulbert Peck, were closed. This was kind of a love affair. Not kind of. I guess he did have a love affair with her in 1908 to 1910. But most importantly, the Wilson papers to 1902 had not yet been

discovered. So it's just as well I did not try to do the …
you know, I sketched out his career, analyzed his historical and political science writings, things like that.

CARROLL: But *The Road to the White House* was received very well. And as you got into the second volume, I guess you decided, "Well, we need more than this."

LINK: Exactly. That's right. Well, the problem was that *The Road to the White House*, particularly beginning about 1907, was written on such a level of detail, that to do this for a president of the United States obviously would require volumes. Which it did require: four more, up until 1917. I had no idea. I thought I'd do two volumes on Wilson. Well, I ended up doing five volumes and got it up to the First World War.

CARROLL: Did you stop there purposely?

LINK: I did not. I stopped there because I got sidetracked, I got derailed on the Wilson papers [publishing project]. In fact, they slightly overlapped. I published the last volume in the biography, *Campaigns for Progressivism and Peace*, in 1964. And by that time we were already heavily at work on the first [published] volume of the Wilson Papers. There was simply no way to do both. Plus, remember I was teaching full time over the period, having a very heavy load of graduate students. I had something like thirty-eight Ph.Ds during my career, and

I was serving on departmental committees. I was very active in the profession … I think I had that old Link energy. And I work pretty hard.

CARROLL: Would there have been one more volume or two more volumes in the Wilson biography after the five you completed?

LINK: There would have been at least four: two volumes on the war, hopefully only one volume on the Peace Conference, although maybe two, and one volume from 1919 to his death. Probably a ten-volume work.

CARROLL: Did you get started on some of those?

LINK: Not really. I have done a bit of article writing, incidental writing, on that later period, a good deal of it. Then other books.

Plus there's no way … I'm getting to a point in my life where I can't go as I did around the world and working from a new source and spending ten years in Washington. I'm too old for that. Somebody will have to finish that.

CARROLL: How did you get involved [as editor of] the Wilson papers? Where were the papers, by the way?

LINK: What were thought to be the papers were in the Library of Congress. Wilson had willed them to the

American people. They were to be deposited in the Library of Congress after Mr. Baker had finished with his biography.

CARROLL: Was Baker allowed to see everything?

LINK: Everything except the letters between the second Mrs. Wilson, I'll call her Edith, and Woodrow. I think he saw everything else. I mean he was allowed to see everything else. He couldn't see everything else by a long shot. There's more than one man could do.

CARROLL: More than *he* could do, not more than what you could do.

LINK: That's right. (Laughs.)

CARROLL: So what were thought to be the papers were at the library. They had been sealed by the family or what?

LINK: Actually, they were left to the Library of Congress. Mrs. Wilson was given the power to say when they should be opened. There was in fact an agreement between Woodrow Wilson and Baker before Wilson died that Baker should have first crack at them, which he did.

Now, I say "thought to be the papers." We'll get back to that.

You asked me about my relationship to the papers, how that got started. Nineteen fifty-six was the centennial year of Wilson's birth, as you know. And the Woodrow Wilson Foundation, which Franklin Roosevelt had helped organize in 1920, 1921, had never had enough money really to be a big mover in any field. They had held some conferences, made some grants and things like that. They led, sponsored the celebrations for Wilson's centennial. And the president of the foundation, Raymond B. Fosdick, was a student of Wilson's, class of 1905, at Princeton, a very close friend. And he was determined that the Woodrow Wilson Foundation with its rather small endowment in those days should devote its entire resources to getting out a fairly complete edition of Wilson's papers. And he's the one really who engineered and powered this whole movement.

So the Wilson Foundation board in 1958 voted to devote its entire resources to getting out a comprehensive edition of Woodrow Wilson's papers.

CARROLL: Little did *they* know.

LINK: Little did they know. And they appointed a committee to select an editor. Arthur Schlesinger, Jr., was on it. August Heckscher [was vice chairman] and Philip C. Jessup were [some of] the people on it. [Other members included Fosdick as chairman, Jonathan Daniels, Harold

W. Dodds, John B. Oakes, and Francis B. Sayre.] I don't mean to sound self-serving, but I was obviously by that time the one person who knew the materials, who had worked widely with the Wilson materials in that period. So they chose me as editor. I accepted.

CARROLL: How, exactly, did they ask?

LINK: I remember quite well. We met at the Century Club in New York in the spring of 1958. We talked about a lot of things and finally they said, "By the way, would you be willing to be editor of the papers?" Well, I knew there had been a lot of talk about this. And I accepted in one minute, I guess.

CARROLL: Then, little did *you* know.

LINK: (Laughs.) Little did *I* know. But I said, "Look, there is a problem." This was 1958. "I'm going to be Harnsworth Professor of American History at Oxford this coming fall for a year." "Oh, that's all right. That makes no difference at all. You can start in 1959."

Wilson's steamer trunks.

BURIED TREASURES
AND RELIABLE SOURCES

CARROLL: What did editing the papers require?

LINK: My first job was to assemble a team to go through all the materials. We had to go through Xeroxing, cataloging, making indexes, and things like that. And I did have a large team down there for four years, from September 1, 1959, to about November 1, 1963. I was teaching at Princeton full time. I didn't move to Washington. I'd go down about once every week, to check on things, keep things going. And we went through all the obvious stuff and some things that weren't so obvious. For example, we saw 600 private manuscript collections for Wilson, made a good start on World War I materials in the National Archives, went through things like the Tumulty papers, all the cabinet papers, White House files and so on. So by November 1963, we thought we were ready to get started on Volume 1.

Ten days before we moved everything up to Princeton, we got a phone call from the people at the Woodrow Wilson House on S Street [in Washington], saying, "You had better come over." I wasn't there in Washington. Two of my assistants went over. And there were five old steel trunks, just jam-packed, letters, papers – here were the Wilson papers until 1902. Nineteen thousand documents. All the letters from his mother and father, his sisters, his brother, all his high school notebooks, as an undergraduate, all his lecture notes, all of them, from the time he started teaching – annotated, beautifully organized.

Nineteen thousand documents that no one knew had existed. They had been in a very far closet up on the servant floor of the Wilson House. And they were renovating the house, making a complete inventory of everything in front of them. It's, I think, one of the greatest manuscript discoveries of all history.

My associate and assistant editor then, John W. Davidson, and David W. Hurst [went over to the house]. I got a phone call immediately and then I came rushing to Washington.

Oh, it was the greatest excitement of my life. You just can't imagine. Before that time, all the Wilson papers to 1902 were in two boxes in the official collection of the Library of Congress. So I told them, "Boys, don't worry about selection or anything, just Xerox everything and bring it up to Princeton." Which they did.

CARROLL: Mrs. Wilson had died?

LINK: Mrs. Wilson died on Wilson's alleged birthday, December 28, 1961. So this was two years later.

But you know, to a scholar, historian, biographer, there's no thrill in the world equal to seeing a mass of monumentally important papers and knowing that you're looking at them for the first time since they were generated. I've had that experience three or four times, but nothing could be compared to this. I mean, you're just so excited and living on cloud nine for weeks and weeks and weeks, particularly as you read the stuff.

CARROLL: Well, how did you do it? Did you start at the beginning?

LINK: I said, "I'm going to start at the beginning and read everything in chronological order." Which is what I did.

CARROLL: Were there some real surprises in there?

LINK: Yes, I think. Baker had seen something of this, but now we had all [Wilson's] undergraduate essays, all his drafts, the draft of a book he published, all his lecture notes. And we knew that he had been very important in the field of administration, but there were three sets [of drafts]. He revised them three times and here they all were.

… It reminds me of seeing the Asquith papers, Herbert Asquith, the British prime minister, when I was doing volumes three, four, and five in the biography. Our great problem at that time was the fifty-year rule of the British and French foreign offices that you could not see a document until fifty years after it had been written. And fifty years hadn't expired. So I wrote around to all the descendants of people who had been in office in Great Britain and I wrote to Sir North Bonham-Carter, who was Asquith's son-in-law, and said, "Would you mind? I know the Asquith papers are at the Bodleian Library at Oxford and would you mind, please, give me permission to look at them?" And he said, "Oh, by all means, look at them. There's nothing in them anyway."

So I went to Oxford. The same old kind of steel trunks, about twelve, fourteen, fifteen of them. They'd bring them up one at a time. And here were the complete … everything that the prime minister of Great Britain saw from 1913 to 1916 I saw – everything. That was another great thrill. No one had ever seen them. They were still in his trunks. They hadn't been looked at, hadn't been organized or arranged.

And I was given access through a subterranean route, really, to the French foreign ministry archives at about the same time. That was a wild story. There was a French historian who was a professor at the Sorbonne, whose

THE REAL WOODROW WILSON

name was J.B. Duroselle. This was 1961. He was coming to speak at Princeton to the Society for the Study of French History. It was meeting at Princeton. So I wrote to him. I told him I had tried through the cultural attaché, the ambassador, in Philadelphia, to see if I could get access and I couldn't. So he said, "Well, I'm going to the [Princeton] meeting. I'll come about forty-five minutes before and we'll talk." He said, "Yes, yes, I know, and you must get into those papers. Now what we have to do is find a formula that will let you in and keep everybody else out." This is typically Gallic. So I said that would be fine with me.

So I went over and we met Pierre Renouvin, the great dean of northern French historians. And Renouvin said, "Yes, by all means you must see them." So then we met the archivist of the foreign ministry and he said, "What we will do is give you a private room back in the stacks. No one will know you're there and you can have complete run of any materials. But you can't quote from them and you can't cite them. You can say in your preface that you've been given access to a very important French diplomatic archive." So I said, "That's better than nothing." So I spent several summers in Paris. And that again, no one had seen these. No one had written anything at all on the subject. So those were the three big thrills of my lifetime.

CARROLL: So now, you've got to start over again on Volume 1.

LINK: Just imagine what would have happened had we published Volume 1. We'd gone down to about 1895. We would have said, "Please folks, throw it away. This is the real Volume 1."

CARROLL: How did you decide what was a Wilson paper and what was not?

LINK: That is the major question: what constitutes a Wilson document? What constitutes a Washington document or a Jefferson document? I worked out I think a definition that's been pretty well accepted in the editing profession. That is, any document generated by Wilson is obviously a Wilson document. Any Wilson speech, anything that he generated either orally or in a written form. Now that doesn't mean you print them all.

CARROLL: You did not?

LINK: Oh no, gracious. Any document, any letter, speech, report, memorandum, congressional report, diplomatic dispatch, anything of that nature that Wilson saw, read – and you have to be sure about this – and had an impact or influence on him is a Wilson document. This is very important. Because without that background and context of what he was reading…. Incidentally, I somewhat redefined the concept of a document. I'd say there are at least twenty-four or twenty-five important diaries for the presidential period. And particularly for the Peace Conference. There are probably twelve to fourteen very important diaries for the Peace Conference, all of which recount sometimes at great length conversations with Wilson. Now is this a Wilson document? Yes, absolutely. Any document that sheds light on his thinking, his formation of policy, on his personality, on his religious views, anything like that is a Wilson document. To give you another example: Wilson as is well known was his own secretary of state, but he was also his own diplomatist and carried on diplomacy in the Oval Office with foreign ambassadors, keeping no record on them himself, none whatsoever. But having hundreds of conferences with foreign ambassadors. But of course these people, all of them distinguished, experienced reporters, would immediately report to their foreign office the conversations. That's a Wilson document. It's absolutely of top importance. There was some criticism at the beginning, some suggestion I was casting too wide a net, but everyone agrees now that this is one of the great features of the Wilson Papers. It includes not just Wilson letters.

See, the old-fashioned way was to go and – let's take the so-called Wilson papers – and you print them, edit them, annotate them and that's it. That's what [John C.]

Fitzpatrick did with George Washington in thirty-nine volumes and that was it. Well, first of all, we couldn't do that with Wilson because so much stuff was missing. We had to get the Wilsons to open up the papers anyway.

But what we have is a record, not complete by any means, but as far as Wilson is concerned, fairly complete, of all materials published, a record of all materials.

We defined what a Wilson document is. You can't print everything – do you want to print everything? … Well, I don't think anybody in his right mind would want to. Again, I think I worked out the formula to serve as a guide for this, that we will print anything of enduring historical significance. Now, you take the White House files, particularly, those not in [the published] Wilson [papers]. Wilson kept his own private files up in his office in the private quarters of the White House. Then you had the vast files, 675 boxes, of files in the executive offices. Well, in addition, you've got the letter books. These are copies – you know how they used to make letterpress copies, hang them up to dry and so on? – of every letter that Wilson dictated and signed. And I would say, just going by the number of letters, that I should think we printed about forty percent of Wilson's letters. Sometimes we printed routine letters just to show that Wilson … for example, he might write to Colonel

[Edward Mandell] House saying, a three-liner, "I just read your memorandum today. Really, it's very important. I'm looking forward to seeing you." I mean, you have thousands and thousands of routine acknowledgments. He would give to his private stenographer, a two-line, three-line form. "Thank you so much for your letter. I derive great encouragement from it, sincerely…."

CARROLL: Then you printed all this, and all the ambassadorial cables?

LINK: We published most of those. If it's important enough for Wilson to call the British ambassador over or for the British ambassador to ask for a conference, it's going to be important enough to print it.

CARROLL: Did you have any idea at the beginning that it was going to be like this, so many documents?

LINK: Yes, I did. Because, you see, I had worked through most of the important stuff down to 1917 before I started on the Wilson Papers. That gave us, literally I think, a ten-year start on the whole project. We didn't have to thrash about trying to find things. I knew where things were, or most things, not everything. This would be 1958, or 1960…. I had not seen these ambassadorial reports yet, but I knew they existed. Some of them had been printed.

Now, the big problem with Wilson is that he rarely ever dictated an important letter. He wrote it on his own typewriter. He never made a single copy of anything he wrote. Now the journalists of that day were largely responsible for this because he started to dictate his letters, and what they would do is put this damp rice paper over it, roll it, and hang it up to dry. And reporters would just roam through the offices reading all the important letters and they'd be published in the *New York Times* the next day.

CARROLL: You're kidding. They had that kind of access?

LINK: They did, yeah – just roaming back and forth, checking letters, literally publishing them the next day in the *New York Times*.

Well, Wilson after that never dictated a letter he wasn't willing to have published in the *New York Times* or the *Washington Post*.

CARROLL: Was there an incident that stopped him?

LINK: It was in April or May 1913. It was a letter to Bryan about the Mexican situation. He would write … well, one day he wrote twelve fairly long letters to Bryan during the *Lusitania* crisis. I would say on the whole he wrote ten to twenty important letters on his typewriter every day. He was a pretty good typist. He used an old – did you ever see an old Hammond typewriter?

CARROLL: Yeah, isn't that in the Wilson House?

LINK: Yes, there's one in the house and one in the White House, too. And he could go pretty fast. He was on the whole an excellent typist. And he'd just bang 'em out and no one knew it. Well, the really important ones he would write out in shorthand before, and then he'd just copy it from the shorthand. As a boy, he taught himself the most difficult system of shorthand ever invented: the Graham system, it's a refinement of Pitman. Very difficult. By sheer two, three years of hard work he taught himself the system.

For example, I'm sure he wrote … now, he didn't write many of his speeches, but he wrote the important ones. I'm sure he wrote the Fourteen Points address in an hour. He had a mind that was so disciplined and so well organized that he could literally tape all that up in his brain and then he'd write in shorthand and then sit down and make a typed copy, a few minor changes, give it to his secretary to have a final copy typed.

CARROLL: And looking at his shorthand, you can see that?

LINK: Oh, yes, you can indeed, yeah. Wilson had a photographic memory and he had the best-organized mind of any person I've ever encountered in history. He had the ability to take a great quantity of material, digest it, organize it, and then work from that, whether a speech or state paper or whatever.

One of our main problems was his speeches, because he rarely wrote any of them in advance.

CARROLL: So you had to work through newspapers – and were those reliable?

LINK: Very good question. First, his private stenographer, Charles Lee Swem, very carefully kept all his shorthand notebooks, all his transcripts, and he cleaned out Wilson's wastebasket every morning or every afternoon – drafts that Wilson had discarded and so on, so the Swem collection at Princeton is of monumental importance.

Now, Swem was an excellent reporter and stenographer. He became one of the great Gregg specialists, what they called the reporting style that's very abbreviated. Swem's problem was, let's say, the campaign of 1912, 1916, anytime, you name it. Wilson's on the road and [Swem's] got to get copy out. Poor fellow. Wilson makes a speech, let's say, at nine o'clock at night. [Swem] would rush to his hotel room and bang out a transcript. And try to get it on the wires, which he does, usually. Sometimes he just can't do it. But he had to do it so quickly he made a lot of mistakes. Now, what do you do?

Well, first of all, I found a man named Jack Romagna, who had been a shorthand reporter for Franklin Roosevelt, [Harry] Truman, and [Dwight] Eisenhower, taken all their press conferences, everything. After looking for, gosh, it was something like thirty-one years, I finally found this man who could read Swem's shorthand. Because that reporting style had not been taught since the 1920s.

What we would do: first of all, you [looked at] Swem's transcript of a speech in Des Moines, Iowa, [or] Minneapolis. You read the transcript against Swem's own shorthand. He was very good. You could make at least in an hour speech, I would say, 300 corrections. You can't stop there, because everywhere Wilson went, his speeches would be reported in full, say in the *Indianapolis News*. And oftentimes, these were real pros, these journalists were. They were a lot better than Swem. So then you have, say, two local versions of the Indianapolis speech. Then you have to read both of those against the corrected Swem transcript. And I had to do this myself, I couldn't trust anyone else. But I would say we probably printed 500, 600 Wilson speeches. Wilson wrote probably not more than twenty-five of those in advance.

Now there was a period in New Jersey, 1911, when you didn't have Swem. Oftentimes, in the New Jersey newspapers, you'd get just a totally corrupt transcript. What do you do? That's the only transcript in existence. Well, I got thinking about this and the thought occurred to me: put that transcript back into the original language in which it was written, that is back into Gregg shorthand, and see what happens. This reporter will have Wilson saying, "The support of the American people is a generous, wonderful support." It's crazy, he couldn't have said that. You put it back into Gregg shorthand. The symbol for "spirit" and "support" are the same. "S-p-r-t" are the sounds. So you could actually retranslate the speech. We had to do a lot of that in 1911.

CARROLL: Wow. That's detective work.

LINK: That's detective work, yeah. Then Swem, who was a very fine person, but Swem had gone only through the fifth grade and had a rather limited vocabulary. He was a boy from out in the country near Trenton. He did go to Ryder Business College, that's where he learned his shorthand. But his vocabulary was somewhat limited. And there are two major mistakes in the official version of Wilson's first inaugural.

I'll give you one example, the most important. (He recites from memory.) Wilson said, "We have erected here a polity that has been the envy of free peoples throughout the world." Swem said, "There's no such word, he didn't mean 'polity,' he meant 'policy.'" So the official version has Wilson saying, "We have erected here a policy…." Well, that doesn't make sense. You can't erect a policy. It's not good grammar. And actually, in this case, we had Wilson's own typed copy, which of course said "polity." But that happened quite a few times. (Laughs.)

It got very tedious.

CARROLL: I was going to say – to do this level of detail and work, didn't you have moments when you thought, "I'm never going to make it through all of this?"

LINK: Yeah, you did. Because most people think that editing is just hijinks and excitement every day. But let me assure you that eight-five percent of the work that you do, that I did at least, was sheer tedium. Comparing transcripts to speeches….

Reading proofs, I insisted that every page of copy that we sent to Princeton [University] Press be read, that the document be read out loud and I would follow the copy, the transcript. Every comma, quotation mark, capitalization, had to be read out loud. It's the only way you can be sure that you're going to get it right. There's no way the human eye can do this unless something comes in between and … mistakes occur all the time. You do know how that is, don't you?… But that's just the beginning.

You send the copy down, you get galley proofs. And those galley proofs have to be re-read at least five or six times. I read every galley.

CARROLL: And you had to read them out loud against the transcripts?

LINK: Read them out loud against the transcripts, that's right. It has to be done. Then the page proofs – you didn't have to do that out loud. Because you can just follow the corrections on the side to be sure the corrections were made.

As a consequence, I think – now this sounds like a ridiculous statement – but I know of only two typographical errors in those sixty-nine volumes. I'm sure there are others, but I haven't seen them, let's put it that way.

CARROLL: Where are they?

LINK: One in Volume 8, there's a "that" that's turned around. I forget where the other one is. It's "t-a-h-t" or something like that. How in the world that got by I don't know.

CARROLL: Does that bother you?

LINK: Oh, it does. (Laughs.) My motto around the office was: "Our margin for error has to be zero." (Laughs.) That's what I kept telling them.

Pastel portrait of Wilson in 1906.

WILSON THE MAN

LINK: Family letters – these were the most exciting. Letters from his mother and father. And they wrote every week. Now you could see the dynamics of that family that you'd never seen before. They were enormously revealing. Actually, pretty much all we knew about old Dr. [Joseph Ruggles] Wilson [Sr., Wilson's father] had been a book by Juliette and Alexander George called *Woodrow Wilson and Colonel House*. And they had portrayed Dr. Wilson as actually quite cruel and domineering, who had molded the son into a kind of a rigid … who had no personality of his own apart from his father. And here we see a very different Dr. Wilson: a man who was loving, supportive, realistic, not overly protective. He spoke the truth. When Wilson cut too many classes, he let him know, but always supporting him, always holding him up. And [Wilson's father was] his greatest teacher. Because Wilson never wrote an essay or a book before the 1880s that he didn't first send to his father.

We find a mother who's very over-protective, who's somewhat neurotic, depressed, constantly playing the son against the father and so on. Not a very jolly relationship.

CARROLL: She was jealous of the relationship between the father and son?

LINK: I think so, and a very depressed person. Sensitive, depressed, gloomy. She'd say, "Now, watch out, your father is going to write you a letter, be prepared for it." And the letter would come and it would be, "My darling son, I noticed that you've been put on probation for too many cuts at the University of Virginia Law School. You better watch out. And you know you can do better," and so forth. It's very supportive. I think it's one of the finest relationships between a father and a son, the finest I've ever encountered.

[Wilson had two older sisters, Annie and Marion, and a younger brother, Joseph R. Wilson, Jr.]

CARROLL: Was Woodrow close to his sisters and his brother?

LINK: Extremely so, a very tightly knit family, as families I think were much more in those days. He was constantly, even when he lived in Princeton, he was constantly seeing Annie, who lived in Columbia, because it was also the Woodrow side, Dr. James Woodrow and all the Woodrow connections were there, and he was very fond of them.

Marion and Ross Anderson moved out to Arkansas about 1888, he never saw them after that.

CARROLL: What happened to them?

LINK: They died. They took a train to Memphis, then they took a steamboat down to someplace on the Mississippi, then went up the Red River by steam paddle and then by horse out to the frontier.

CARROLL: They didn't live long after they were out there?

LINK: No, just two years. But they wrote every week. And Wilson saved every letter from all his siblings. Jody, or Joseph Jr., was something of a problem. He was constantly getting into trouble and Wilson was constantly having to get him out of trouble. But he was a loyal brother. He put up with a lot.

CARROLL: If Woodrow Wilson could be sitting in this other chair right now, is there something about him, after all you've read about him, that you would ask, that you still don't know?

LINK: (Long pause.) I think, actually not. While it was certainly true when I started. If you read the end of one chapter, I said only a psychologist could figure out what was going on in Wilson's mind. I think we know a good deal more about the motivations, what he did, than Wilson did himself. And I think that is the thing I'm proudest of.

The characteristic Wilson was a man who exhibited tremendous powers of leadership – and by that I mean getting different groups together and reconciling differences – and finding the medium. He did this, for example, time and again, on the Federal Reserve bill [the Federal Reserve Act, which created the Federal Reserve system], he did it at Princeton, and so on. A man who, though not giving away any essential principles, was always able to bring people together on common ground. That was his great genius.

Now there are two periods in his life when that leadership broke down. One was 1906 to 1910 at Princeton and one was 1919 to 1921 after he got back from Paris, when he, I think, actually prevented ratification of the [Versailles] treaty because of his rigidity in not accepting reservations [what were considered mostly modest changes to the treaty]. Now, how do you explain this? I didn't know him in the beginning. And it was not until we were well along: Wilson had a tremendous retinal accident, some called it a stroke, it certainly was the result of hypertension, when a vein in his left eye exploded and blinded him in his left eye.

CARROLL: Was he permanently blind in that eye?

LINK: Yeah, he had only peripheral vision.

CARROLL: When did that happen?

LINK: May 28, 1906, when he was fifty years old. He had had, I think, what seemed to me to be a small stroke in

1896, when his right arm and his hand were paralyzed for six or eight months. And we started accumulating more and more evidence of this sort. Then finally, the son of Wilson's physician … [Cary Travers] Grayson, opened – you've probably seen that material. But we can now see the whole syndrome. Here's a man who's suffering from very severe hypertension. He certainly appeared to be [in a lacunar state, evidenced by a lack of abstract thinking].

This certainly started in 1906, I think he was already in the lacunar state.

CARROLL: You see a marked change in his ability to …

LINK: … cope, his ability to strategize, his ability to just accomplish his goals. He messes things up by acting like a stroke victim.

Now he has a remarkable remission when he gets into politics. There's a whole change of venue. It's a new world. This is particularly true when he goes to Washington. Dr. Grayson put him – he's a very good doctor by the way – puts him on a simple diet. Wilson loved southern cooking: fried chicken, lots of gravy, and all that. He put him on a simple diet and lots of exercise and low stress as much as possible. That really did wonders for him.

CARROLL: Low stress, as president of the United States.

LINK: That's right, the lowest possible. Particularly two to three hours a day out on the golf course. Or walking, some kind of exercise. Now that worked wonders. Wilson had not had a major stroke before that. He'd had, probably, three or four small strokes. But once we got in the war in the summer of '17 and particularly once mobilization was geared up in 1918 in a big way, he was working twelve or fourteen hours a day.

You can print this: it's the first time it'll ever appear in print. I'm going to start a book on the relationship between Wilson and Grayson. It's a marvelous relationship. Grayson was just like a son to Wilson and Grayson worshiped Wilson and Wilson thought Grayson was one of the finest people he'd ever known. The Grayson family have opened all their father's papers, including letters from Admiral Dr. Grayson to his wife and their mother. In the summer of 1918, as a lot of people did, Mrs. [Alice] Grayson took, well they had just one child at that time, went down to White Sulphur Springs [in West Virginia] for the summer and Dr. Grayson stayed up with Wilson.

And along July 16, Wilson nearly died. July 16, 1918, he said, "We barely saved the president's life today. Only three people in the world know this: Mrs. Wilson, Wilson, and myself" – no, he didn't say Wilson, he said the nurse. He said nobody will ever know this fact, but he nearly died. Well, I talked with a lot of doctors and they said it had to have been cardiac arrest. It couldn't have been an infection, he wouldn't be over it in three or four days – over it in the sense that he's up and about. What else could it have been? It couldn't have been the flu. It couldn't have been a virus.

CARROLL: This is before the major stroke in 1919.

LINK: Oh yes. Long before.

CARROLL: It could have been cardiac arrest?

LINK: Most likely. That's what all the neurologists tell me.

CARROLL: Do the medical records show anything?

LINK: No, except we know Wilson was confined to his room for three or four days. But that's all. I'd never known it. I just discovered it a month ago. Up at the Graysons'.

CARROLL: So this is not known.

LINK: Never appeared in print. Only three or four people know this. Wilson did have a small stroke in Paris on April 28, 1919. I think this has been pretty well established. I didn't discover it. We have clinical evidence on that, the records of the doctors.

CARROLL: The last pictures we see of Wilson are at the S Street house, a kind of feeble, defeated …

LINK: … and never smiling. I was thinking about that the other day. There's not a smile in a picture.

CARROLL: I've seen one somewhere. Kind of a toothy…

LINK: One, yes. The one you saw was a highly doctored picture. We print that in Volume 66 or 67, in 1920. That's one where he's signing a document and Edith is standing by and he's kind of got a smile on his face. That was all just touched up.

CARROLL: But I thought I saw him earlier, throwing out a baseball or something….

LINK: Oh, he smiled constantly.

CARROLL: But we have an image of Wilson as rather severe, long-faced …

LINK: … long-faced….

CARROLL: But he was a practical joker, wasn't he?

LINK: Oh yes. Not only that, a great mimic. A tremendous mimic. Black stories, Irish stories, he was wonderful on Irish stories. Loved to sing. Great jokester. And loved above all limericks. He'd recite them all the time in campaign speeches.

CARROLL: Clean ones.

LINK: Well, usually. He'd say, "There was a monk from Siberia …" – this is the raciest he would ever, this is as far as he'd ever go – "There was a monk from Siberia, whose life grew drearier and drearier; from the depths of his cell, he let out a yell, and eloped with the Mother Superior." (Laughs.) That was the raciest.

CARROLL: When did he do that, at a campaign thing?

LINK: At the cabinet. I don't think he'd say that in public. He could dislocate his jaw and wiggle it ... just to be funny. And he could wiggle his nose and his ears. You'd get the most riotous times in the White House ... no, he was fun, he was kind of a prankster.

CARROLL: This is wholly contrary to what we see ...

LINK: But you see, you were a distinguished man, certainly the president of the United States, you were supposed to look like a distinguished man. I think of a painting of Theodore Roosevelt. You know that tremendous grin? You don't see any of that in his paintings. He was a rather jolly person. But he's very serious. And I can remember back when I was a boy, that's the way my father had his picture taken. You were supposed to look very dignified.

I think the sweetest portraits of Wilson were [made] by Fred Yates of Ambleside and we reproduce them. They're crayon drawings actually made in 1906 and 1908. There are two of them. I have copies of them in my study. They're portraits of Wilson as president of Princeton University. They're very sweet, of Wilson smiling. Of course, these were family property. They weren't known.

Sporting a favorite golf cap, Wilson boards a train, October 12, 1916.

THE REAL WILSON

CARROLL: Did you like Wilson?

LINK: I didn't like him at first.

CARROLL: You didn't like him at first?

LINK: No. Actually, my first image was formed by reading Baker.

CARROLL: But Baker was trying to make him look good.

LINK: But Baker diluted him. He made a priss and a prude out of him. Wilson was an austere Presbyterian. He took ... [from] Dr. [Stockton] Axson [Wilson's] religious convictions and Axson didn't know anything about this. According to Axson, who was Wilson's brother-in-law, Wilson did not believe in an all-merciful God, he believed in a God of the Old Testament, like a Calvinist. That wasn't true. And that didn't set well with me.

But, as I say, we didn't know very much when I first started. Baker, and the William E. Dodd biography, which is a pretty good biography, by the way – politically and historically better than Baker.

I'll tell you when I first saw the real Wilson. It was in his letters to his first wife – 2,800 letters between the two of them, and I think the greatest love correspondence in history as far as I know. As far as I've ever seen. Wilson thought of a thousand ways to say, "I love you." Here you see him, he writes every day when he's away from home. And fortunately he is away a great deal. And he pours out every thought.

And this happens later, his letters to Edith when he was courting her. Fortunately, she was away most of the summer of 1915 before they were married. She was gone for six weeks.

I was the first person to see these letters. She had had them sealed and I talked to her at great length about them. Now Mr. Baker hadn't seen them.

I said, "Now, Mrs. Wilson, you know, these must be wonderful letters." She said, "Yes, but they're too intimate and I'm going to have them burned."

I don't know that she was serious, but she really did say that to me. And I said, "But Mrs. Wilson, let's face it: you and your husband belong to history. You've got to put personal considerations aside. Remember that, particularly your husband. Now, don't these letters reveal a side of him, his capacity for love, his love of people, and a great man of words ... don't all these characteristics that we don't know much about, don't they come out?"

"Oh yes, yes." "Well," I said, "Don't you want the world to know this?" "Well, I guess I do." I said, "Well, I tell you what ..." "Well, I'm so afraid that if I open these let-

ters, someone's going to come along and just trim off …
because he's very frank. They'll just print the sensational
letters and when they do it, perhaps vulgarize them."

And I said, "Tell you what to do: add a codicil to your
deed of gift of your papers to the Library of Congress
and say that" – in point of fact, these were her letters –
"saying that they would not be read, quoted, or seen by
anyone except the editors of the [Wilson] Papers and
then they will all be published and then they will be in
the public domain to be used."

"That's it," she said. "You go home and write that for
me." So I did, I went home and typed it out and sent it to
her, she signed it, she sent it to the Library of Congress.

CARROLL: You didn't see them until she died, then?

LINK: No. Certainly not. He wrote her, he would get up
at six o'clock in the morning and write her a twenty-page
letter until eight o'clock.

CARROLL: Typed or handwritten?

LINK: These were all handwritten. And then, from ten
until midnight, he would write another twenty pages.
Forty pages a day. Describing every single thing that had
happened to him that day. Well, I tell you what. They
were the biggest presidential letters in history. Now it
did come out that he'd confessed to her that he'd had this
affair with Mrs. Peck. And that comes out in his letters

and that's what [Mrs. Wilson] was worried about. And I said, "Well, Mrs. Wilson, you know this is, gracious me, a very small business indeed when you look at the whole picture. I mean, my word, I wouldn't worry about that."

CARROLL: This is when he was married to Ellen?

LINK: To Ellen.

CARROLL: They did not have a happy marriage?

LINK: Oh, they had a supremely happy marriage, but a terrible tragedy happened to her in 1905: her brother, whom she had reared from a little boy six years up, and his wife and child were drowned and she went into a deep depression and, I think, went into her bedroom and locked the door. That's what I think. And Wilson met this lively, vivacious, charming lady… but he fell in love with her. He talked in his letters to Edith, of this summer, his "months of madness and folly." But I think this is important. The important thing is, he wrote to Edith, he said on account of this great transgression – a thing like this would be a terrible sin to a man of conscience – "I decided I would devote the rest of my life to the service of other people." So I think in a way it was a turning point in his life. Good came out of what was not….

CARROLL: He went back to his spiritual training….

LINK: Exactly.

CARROLL: He felt he had to make amends.

LINK: He had to make amends for his sin. I think, like Jimmy Carter, if he lusted after a woman in his heart that would be a sin. He had just a highly developed conscience.

But anyway, I think she probably would have died and not done anything about those letters. And she had left explicit orders they were to remain sealed. I think they would still be sealed. I think we would have had to get a court order or something. Who knows?

CARROLL: ...You say you didn't like Wilson at first, but it was the love letters, that you would have been reading in 196-...

LINK: Mrs. Eleanor Wilson McAdoo gave all those letters, most of them, to the Princeton Library, to our collection, in October 1961.

CARROLL: Boy, were you around at the right moments.

LINK: Around at the right moments. We had a little ceremony and presentation and a dinner and so on. Dr. Fosdick drew me to one side and said, "Arthur, I want you to know that Eleanor" – and he was kind of a father [to her] – "told me she destroyed 350 of the letters that were just too intimate."

Well, I got to thinking. Well, what happened? Those letters, Mr. Baker had them and he turned all that stuff over to the Library of Congress and then Wilson had provided in his will that Eleanor should get these letters. So they first must have come to the Library of Congress manuscript division, then would have sent them by express to California, Santa Barbara, where she was living. Then she would have destroyed these letters. Now, there's no way, I said to myself, that they could have sent those across the continent without making …

CARROLL: Copies!

LINK: Copies. Without making at least a microfilm copy. So the head of the manuscript division was on my editorial advisory committee. I called him up. I said, "Look, didn't you make a microfilm copy?" He said: "It's complete." I said: "How about giving me a copy?" He said: "Sure, be glad to." So … (chuckles). There are ways of getting around things like that.

CARROLL: When did you see those then?

LINK: 1961.

CARROLL: And that's when you began to see …

LINK: I began to see, I mean, literally, for a couple of years when he's courting her, and he's immediately, a totally different kind of person.

CARROLL: There's the human …

LINK: … the human side. I wouldn't want this put in print, but Wilson was a very romantic, he was a great lover. He's the greatest lover we ever had as president. You can say that. But he was also the most highly sexed.

CARROLL: Really?

LINK: No, no. He can't compare to Kennedy. But he was a highly sexed man. And the nice thing is – this is why I say Baker denuded him – you wouldn't get this from Baker. He would discuss sexual functions with his wives quite openly and candidly. He'd say, "This is a wonderful gift of God, why should we be so covered about it?"… A lot of these letters are very frank.

CARROLL: These have all been published in the papers?

LINK: Every single one.

CARROLL: Where?

LINK: Particularly in the 1890s. He gets very … because he's separated….

CARROLL: So it's early on.

LINK: Very early on. He starts in 1888 going down to Johns Hopkins University [in Baltimore] to give these lectures on administration for six weeks every winter…. Then he's away from his wife at least until the weekends. And he can't go back every weekend. So he's writing letters. And he builds up quite a lot of …

CARROLL: Energy.

LINK: (Laughs.) Energy and passion. And then he does occasionally go off for a day visit or night visit, like that.

Flowers along Wilson's way, Dover, England, December 27, 1918.

WILSON AND PEACE

LINK: Actually, the hardest thing that we did, and certainly the hardest thing I did, was the Paris Peace Conference. We devoted about twelve volumes to it and six years of very hard work. And I thought we would never get out of Paris, frankly. Wilson was there six months and we were there six years. But the problem was, that the documentation, that conference went on for six months. It started January 18 through June 28.

CARROLL: Wilson was there that whole time....

LINK: He was there most of it. He went home in the middle of the conference in February 1919.

But Wilson was there in his own little palace. And Swem was there. And everything was kept. The papers of the American Commission to Negotiate Peace. That's about three million items. Now that doesn't mean you have to look through three million, but you've got to know what's there. Plus all the English and all the French materials.

CARROLL: What about German materials?

LINK: Well, there wasn't a lot of German. They didn't come until very late. Some German, but not much. Because they were there, they came May 5 and left June 28.

CARROLL: You speak and read French?

LINK: Yes, I'm quite fluent in French. Fortunately, one of my associate editors was German and bilingual. I did all the French work. In fact, the thing I'm proudest of is my... did you ever see my translation and edition of the [Paul] Mantoux notes of the Council of Four? Princeton [University] Press published them [in 1992] in two volumes. The Council of Four was born March 24 at Wilson's suggestion and everything came up to the Council of Four. The French interpreter kept a virtually verbatim record of all the conversations. In fact, of the first thirty-eight sessions, that's our only record of the conversations. Then they brought in an official secretary who started taking decisions. That's what they had to have. The French interpreter was named Mantoux, who published his transcripts in two volumes in a very limited, small edition in 1955, called *Les Délibérations du Conseil de Quatre*. They'd never been translated except for just a few of the sessions. So I translated them, with a lot of help, but I did the translation, all right. I decided to make it a self-contained unit. It's very heavily annotated. For example, they're discussing a draft of a proposed article in the treaty with Germany. And there's some line, so and so, and then as an appendix, I'll print that draft so you can turn right to it. It's kind of self-contained. It gives you marvelous views of every important thing and a lot of very unimportant things that came before the Council of Four.

CARROLL: So here you have sixty-nine volumes of Wilson stuff and you couldn't quit.

LINK: I couldn't quit.... Well, you do it by just sticking at it and by not fooling around. This is a terrible thing to say about oneself, but I think I do have an unusual ability to concentrate ... and I keep my mind on what I'm doing. You've got to look forward to every day as something really exciting and tremendous is going to happen that day. And go to work with that feeling. Also, a great deal of weekend work. I worked every Saturday and usually every Sunday afternoon.

... But my great discovery was [Wilson] had a really bad, small stroke on July 19, 1919, which had never been known.

CARROLL: A year and three days after ...

LINK: ... after he nearly died. He was in Washington. He had just got back from Paris. He got back on July 8. He presented the treaty to the Senate on July 10. He was in very bad shape at that time. I'm building up toward this. For example, writing that speech to the Senate presenting the treaty. He had the hardest time writing that speech. He worried about it on the boat coming back. He hadn't done a thing on that speech when he got back and he finished it only three hours before he went before the Senate. And it's not a good speech. It's a terrible speech. That was July 10, then nine days later …

Well, the day before, he sees Sir William Wiseman, who was attached to [intelligence in] the British Embassy, and he says, "I know there are going to have to be some reservations to the treaty, but we'll work them out and we're going to get this thing through."… That was a Friday. July 19 was a Saturday. And there were all kinds of rumors of an impending great storm coming up the river, and Dr. Grayson hustles Wilson off on the *Mayflower*, the presidential yacht, to take him down to Chesapeake Bay. And he's out for about a week. That was really, I think …

CARROLL: He sent him out even though there was a storm?

LINK: Yeah.

CARROLL: So, get him seasick too?

LINK: I don't know what happened. He told reporters he had dysentery, bad water in the White House.... Anyhow, I think that stroke was more important than the big one on October 2.

CARROLL: Why was that?

LINK: The reason is, there was a group of seven moderate and very distinguished Republican senators. Frank Kellogg of Minnesota, Albert B. Cummins of Iowa, and so on, who had come forward with four very simple, moderate reservations. And Wilson in fact later virtually copied them. Here was Wilson's choice: the only way you could get that treaty through was to get a bipartisan coalition. You've got to get two-thirds plus one vote in the Senate for approval before the president can then go ahead with ratification. They were offering this olive branch to Wilson and a healthy, characteristic Wilson would have snapped at, would have jumped at the opportunity. He would have had those men come to the White House [and said], "Let's get together, work this thing out, and get this treaty through." And in fact that was always a possibility.

But not after that stroke of July 19. It so discombobulated him he lost his memory, lost his poise, and so on. And never was an effective leader after that. His leadership just crumbled and crumbled and crumbled. Now the massive stroke of October 2 absolutely, of course, doomed the treaty because, in the first place, Wilson was really just not functioning physically and mentally. I'd say October 2 not more than five or eight percent I would say, until February 1. Then when he did start functioning a little bit, it was a disaster. Because he was a typical post-stroke victim – rigid, uncompromising, unyielding, incapable of abstract thinking: can we do it this way? can we do it that way? and so forth. And he made it a partisan issue in the Jackson Day Dinner [speech]. And then, an awful letter to Senator [Gilbert M.] Hitchcock on March 8 [1920]. That was the most important presidential letter in American history. That letter made it absolutely inevitable that the treaty would go down to defeat.

CARROLL: What did he say?

LINK: He would not accept any reservations and he lunged out at the British and French governments – in a public letter – accusing them of being imperialistic and militaristic and taking a very high ground, that only the United States could give the moral leadership that the world needed, and the rest of the world was so corrupt that they don't expect...

CARROLL: Why did people around Wilson allow him to go that far?

LINK: Well, here's the way it worked. Wilson dictated drafts, three or four drafts, and the only person who saw them was Tumulty, his so-called secretary, chief of staff. Now Tumulty to his credit in January had worked very hard to get a compromise. And in fact had drafted a letter from Wilson to Hitchcock, who was Wilson's spokesman, Gilbert M. Hitchcock of Nebraska, in the Senate, which was circulated among the cabinet members. It was a marvelous letter accepting most of the reservations and, by George, Wilson just nearly went with it, and then something happened. What happened was, he had little spell of flu in late January and recovered about February 1 and along with this recovery came a kind of surge of energy, almost like encephalitis, kind of a fantasy, a brain disease, and he just kept the whole thing with him, and had nothing to do with it.

CARROLL: What did Tumulty say to him? "Mr. President, you're making a huge mistake." Could they tell him that? Were they afraid of him?

LINK: No, Tumulty was not afraid of him. He told him the truth. He told him the truth in correspondence and I'm sure he saw him every day at that time. He must have said, "Mr. President, you know you're throwing away the best chance…." He did, in fact, in a letter, that would be in Volume 64 or 65, the correspondence is there, that draft letter is there. [Secretary of State Robert]

Lansing wrote him. He said: "If this letter is sent, the treaty will be ratified." [He meant] the January letter.

The one in March, I'll say this to Tumulty's credit: he was so loyal. What he did was, Wilson actually in his first draft was very disparaging to Marshal [Ferdinand] Foch and President [Raymond] Poincaré by name in a public letter. Tumulty got all that cleaned up. But it was still, it was bad enough.

CARROLL: Wilson was determined: "I want this letter sent."

LINK: That's what he said. It was sent.

CARROLL: Telling me this story kind of runs counter to what the public knows about Wilson. The public is under the impression that Edith was running the show.

LINK: Nonsense. That was nonsense.... She made two important political decisions. Dr. Grayson and his chief consultant, Dr. Francis X. Durkham of Philadelphia, Jefferson Medical College, wanted to make a full report and disclosure what had happened to Wilson about October 18. And so Grayson had Dr. Durkham – you'll see this in Volume 64 – write up his notes of his first three or four examinations of Wilson, from October 2, 3, 4, and 5, something like that. And they're very full, complete. And, you don't want this detail, but I did submit these reports to two of the top stroke people in the country, and they said: "We could hardly do better today. This is just magnificent." And this is what Wilson had.

Anyhow, Mrs. Wilson vetoed publication and said, "Absolutely not." Now what was poor Grayson to do? There's a patient-doctor relationship. It's absolutely privileged. And sacred. Then Dr. Grayson on January 15 persuaded Wilson to resign. And in fact, Wilson had even drafted notes about when to go to the Senate. That was kind of fantasy, because he couldn't get out of bed hardly. But, anyhow, Mrs. Wilson absolutely vetoed this. She said, "Where are we going to live? The White House is an awfully nice place to live. And you're well taken care of."

Those are the only two important political decisions she made.

I talked to her many times about this. I got to know her quite well in the last three or four years of her life. She would always say, "Well, how in the world could I run the government of the United States and I knew nothing about running a government and I wasn't even interested in politics?" Which was true. She had no interest in political matters. The departmental heads ran the departments, on the whole quite well. Tumulty was the organizer. And when Wilson got able, he'd take things and show them to him. Now things would be sent, Tumulty would give things to Mrs. Wilson to read to Wilson. He had double vision in his right eye during this period and couldn't read. And he would often – she'd write on the side: "The president says he simply doesn't have strength enough to deal with this. It's going to have to be deferred."

There were a lot of outstanding diplomatic problems. Poor Lansing was "This or that?" and Wilson just put him off. No action. "The president's not strong enough." Or he'd put it aside.

Tumulty and the department heads ran the government. And as I say, on the whole, well, except for [Attorney General Mitchell] Palmer, who went on that looney Red rampage, you remember the Palmer raids? Wilson didn't know anything about it. I don't think Wilson ever knew about the Palmer raids.

CARROLL: … At the time he left office, what did the public know about his illness?

LINK: Everything. After the failure of his initiative by Grayson, the disclosure document, Grayson always said, "Wilson is a very sick man, and he has to be very careful." But someone said, "It's been reported by Senator [George Higgins] Moses of New Hampshire that the president's had a stroke." And he said, "Well, is Senator Moses a doctor?" He never said yes or no. But things like this can't be kept quiet. Everybody in the know in Washington had known within two weeks. Everybody on the Hill. The Republicans, I'm sure they were very sorry that this had happened to Wilson, but they didn't want to stir things up. After all, they had a majority in Congress and it was politically to their advantage to have Wilson on the flat of his back. Why bring in somebody who might be able to do something? The Democrats couldn't come out openly. But Wilson at the time of his stroke, he had a blockage in his urethra, and they called in Dr. Anthony Young of Johns Hopkins, a urologist, a very distinguished man. The question was whether to operate – if that had happened, he probably would have died – or see if nature couldn't solve the problem, which it did. But Dr. Young, in an interview, February 20, said: "We all agreed at the time that the president had had a thrombosis in the brain and suffered a stroke." And that really let the cat out of the bag, although as I say, that wasn't all that much news. People knew that, my Lord.

CARROLL: Did the people know that?

LINK: They knew he was very, very ill because Grayson said so. He said, "He's a very sick man and there's a chance that he may not survive. And he cannot have any burdens laid on him, he cannot do anything."

CARROLL: Vice President Thomas R. Marshall was not a force at all?

LINK: (Shakes head.) Unfortunately. He had a great fear of assassination.

CARROLL: Of Wilson's assassination?

LINK: Of his succeeding and then somebody killing him. He was in Atlanta making a speech when a report came that Wilson had died, and he fainted. (Laughs.)

CARROLL: So he wasn't ready….

LINK: He didn't want to be president.

Now Grayson I think was very frank with the cabinet. We don't know what he said. He didn't say, "The president's had a devastating stroke." He said, "He's a very sick man and it's going to be months before he's able to function again." In other words, he's disabled, constitutionally. Now it's up to the cabinet to take the leadership in arranging a succession. And that's what Lansing wanted to do. Lansing was absolutely right. Tumulty was desirous, because of the emotionalism thing, "Don't dare do that because the crippled leader is lying there, on his back in the White House, we can't be that disloyal." And there was nobody else in the cabinet willing to do what had to be done. I blame the leading Democratic senators who knew what the situation was. Carter Glass,

Hitchcock was a very weak man. Hitchcock of all people because he saw Wilson a couple of times. He knew how sick he was.

CARROLL: No one did anything.

LINK: No one did anything and just saw the whole treaty go to smithereens. Rather than take the simple steps to have him declared disabled, Congress could have done that by joint resolution.

CARROLL: Then Marshall …

LINK: Then Marshall would have been acting president, but with all the powers of the president. And the treaty would have gone through. Wilson would probably have been reinstated around October 1920 when he was better. But nobody had the courage to do it.

Arthur S. Link and his work, 1993.

THE LEGACY OF
WILSON AND HIS PAPERS

LINK: The project brought me into contact with hundreds of very interesting people. Not just the Wilson biography, but the whole Wilson period, 1910 to 1921. It's undoubtedly the most important period in the whole twentieth century. It's the most important ten years. It set the structure for all the events that were to follow. For example, it made the Second World War inevitable. Not because the Treaty of Versailles was a bad treaty, by any means, but because in my opinion it wasn't stringent enough. But, also looking on the brighter side, it marked the most important turning point in the direction of American government and the American people in world affairs.

CARROLL: We got in and were never getting out.

LINK: There's no way you can get out once you get in. In spite of the rejection of the treaty, we still went to war in 1941. And would have gone to war if the Japanese hadn't attacked us.

Also, out of that dreadful experience in the First World War – much more dreadful, from the British and French and German and American viewpoint than that of the Second World War – we didn't lose as many men, we weren't in it long enough, but look what the French and British and Italians lost alone – out of that experience did come a conviction that mankind somehow has to find a better way than wars like this. Now, the League of Nations did not prevent the Second World War, but in an enterprise so ambitious and so grand in its scale, that is, organizing for peace and preventing war, you don't achieve that goal, that aim, overnight, you don't achieve it in ten, twenty, thirty years, you may achieve it in fifty, sixty, a hundred years. And I think we're on our way to achieving it. That's when people are starting to say, "No way, the human race cannot survive if this goes on." And I am optimistic, yes. I think great things like this do take a century, maybe more, for fulfilment, culmination.

CARROLL: And Wilson put it on the track.

LINK: He put it on the track. And that's what he said, he says, "It's an infant." "An infant has been born, a precious thing has been born. Now we have to nurture it into manhood, and it's going to take a long time." And we're still working at it. But, my Lord, look at NATO and OAS … and now the United Nations is actually doing something. But it's going to take a while. It's not perfect.

But I think the Gulf War is really a perfect model for what a really united, purposeful UN can do if it will do it. And they have to do it. The historical necessity pulls them to it. And I think the Japanese writer of *The End of History*, [Francis] Fukuyama, I think he's fundamentally right, that the whole world is moving, all the great powers are all moving onto the same political plane, of democracy and constitutional government and so on. Democracies don't go to war with one another, not usually.

CARROLL: … But that Hitchcock letter set everything on the course to World War II. With the League, it would have been entirely different.

LINK: I think so. That's speculative history and what they call counterfactual history because it didn't happen and we didn't get the League. I think it would have made all the difference in the world, particularly in the reparations problem.

CARROLL: What are some of your other discoveries from these papers?

LINK: I think one thing would be Wilson's very astounding knowledge of economics, certainly macroeconomics and to some degree microeconomics, for that day. Also, he was a very distinguished scholar. I think we had all just absolutely downgraded him unmercifully.

CARROLL: Even after writing a five-volume *History of the American People,* he didn't have a credential?

LINK: No, he didn't really, before these papers came [to light]. Of course, you can see how he's building and building and we printed a little of his bibliographies and lot of his stuff like that which shows how careful a scholar he was. And, in fact, [he was] most creative and imaginative and bold in his interpretations. And I think one of the founders of political science and American history, of the professional study of it. That was pretty new.

But I think his grasp of economics kind of shook me up. You know, he taught – he didn't advocate it – he knew Karl Marx. He had read Karl Marx, *Das Capital*. He knew his Marx and he knew all the current literature.

He pretty well in his own mind constructed the whole structure of the Federal Reserve system. He had that outlined in his mind by October 1912. He had a long discussion with [Edward Mandell] House.

CARROLL: It was set up during his time?

LINK: Right. If you look at the [Wilson] papers, there's a long press conference, I think it's June 21, 1915, where they talk about the bill and its particulars and whole questions of money supply and this and that and I was just absolutely astounded to think he had a mastery of that sort of micro[economics]....

… You know I wrote a lot of history, not just Wilson. I have never encountered a person – let's say a political person; that's very important because there are others – [who] read so widely in so many fields and who in very important things was able to get right to the root of matters.

For example, he was an absolutely first-class theologian to my mind, a brilliant preacher, but he stands up today, I mean, he is vastly above any other. He was a professional theologian.

CARROLL: I remember a small book Wilson wrote called *The Minister and the Community*.... And now you've got [another book on Wilson].

LINK: … I edited [it].... Stockton Axson did a partial biography of Wilson, which I called *Brother Woodrow*.... It's a marvelous thing. He knew him longer than any other person except Wilson's father and brother. He was Ellen Wilson's brother and lived with the Wilsons for long periods. I guess along with Grayson and Wilson's father, Stockton Axson was really the closest friend Wilson ever had. He was kind of like a son, because he spent long periods with Mr. Wilson.

CARROLL: Rich in detail….

LINK: Yes, rich in personal detail.

CARROLL: It was never published?

LINK: It was never published because he dictated the thing and he was so lazy that he never got around to putting it all together and revising it.

CARROLL: And you came across this during your editing of the papers?

LINK: Yes. He and Grayson were going to get out a joint biography. And this was Axson's part and Grayson never did his. A little bit. Grayson did a marvelous thing on the personality of Wilson and then a chapter on the Big Four, which I will use.

And there are three or four drafts. So I tried to get the best version possible. I didn't make anything up or anything like that. I used Axson's own words. It actually was with the Graysons' help that they gave it to me.

CARROLL: That was a nice find.

LINK: That was a nice find indeed.

CARROLL: … I'm thinking about other presidential papers projects: Franklin Roosevelt's papers, then Fitzpatrick's work on Washington….

LINK: That's a good job, except it's not annotated. And, of course, it's not complete….

CARROLL: … Who did you use as a model, or did you think, "I'll have to create my own model?" [John] Nicolay and [John] Hay on Lincoln [1890] – I don't know what you think of them….

LINK: I think it's good. I think on the whole, reliable and excellent.

CARROLL: But you had no modern model?

LINK: No, except the [Elting E.] Morison [editing of the] letters of Theodore Roosevelt. I thought they were beautifully annotated. Now, mind you, they're just eight volumes. And as it turned out, a lot of new material turned up. And they're just Roosevelt letters, no incoming letters. But what they did I thought they did awfully well. They were kind of a model for me for annotation. But not for selection. Taking it as a whole, I had no model for the project. You know, I was not trained, although I'd done a bit of editing, a little bit, but not a book or anything like that.

Actually, the kind of work you do as an editor is the kind of work you do as a writer. It's different. But the historical [work] and methodology is the same. You should be as careful in writing a biography in your quotations and your citations as we have to be in a great edition like the Wilson Papers. I have never yet published a book where I did not go back and check every footnote, every quotation. There's just some simple rules that apply to all historical work. I thought the big problem is the problem of annotation, how much annotation should you have, and selection. Those are the two big problems. And here it's a matter of self-confidence. And fortunately, I'd been working with Wilson for eighteen to twenty years before I really got involved in the Wilson Papers, so by that time if I didn't have a good deal of confidence and didn't think I could do a pretty good job, I certainly wouldn't have done it. I think that's the key to the way in which we got volumes out. A little over two volumes a year.

CARROLL: Princeton and the Wilson Foundation did this together?

LINK: No, the Wilson Foundation actually paid the outright costs: salaries, Xeroxing, things like that. Princeton furnished marvelous facilities, paid my salary during all that time, and also did all our bookkeeping, so that we never had to worry about a thing from that side. And there's a nice little ending to this story. The Wilson Foundation started out with a little over a million dollars in endowments when we started. And actually Dr. Fosdick got from the Ford and Mellon foundations something like $700,000 to do the first big research job, which took four years. Without that, I don't think we could have ever gotten this off the ground. Right now, through wise investment and careful management, the endowment of the Woodrow Wilson Foundation is over $13 million. For many years, we didn't spend all the income.

CARROLL: Do you know who is purchasing the Woodrow Wilson Papers? Are they a bestseller?

LINK: Yes, for a series like this, they are. They sell around 2,000 copies within five or six years, [that's for] each volume. And the first volume has sold about 7,000 copies. I think you could say every good college and university in the world has a set. Almost every one. Now, one reason I know this is from first-hand observation. I go to Warsaw and they take me into the Warsaw National Library and they take me back in the stacks and show me the Wilson Papers. I go to a provincial Danish university library and the librarian takes me back and shows me the Wilson Papers. I know there are several sets in Moscow and St. Petersburg over in Russia, although they were withheld from the graduate students for a long time. They are now open. I had this experience: when we were closing up the office in March or April 1992, I had an extra set, my working set. I wanted to give it to a good college. And I wrote around to twenty-five or thirty colleges, saying wouldn't you like a set? And every one of them said, "No, we've been buying the Wilson Papers ever since they had been published." I just couldn't find a good college that didn't have a set of the Wilson Papers.

CARROLL: So what did you do with that set?

LINK: I gave that set along with my library, about 3,000 books over a fifty-year period, to a fine, little college, out about seven miles from here, Warren Wilson College. It's a Presbyterian work-study college. No relation to Woodrow Wilson. It has about 800 or 900 students. It started out as a mission college to mountain students. And it's turned into a lovely, good little college. So that's what happened to them.

CARROLL: What did you feel like when you were closing up the office? Did you know it would go as long as it would go?

LINK: Mmmm, yeah. I knew within five years.

CARROLL: What did your wife [Margaret Douglas Link] think of this?

LINK: She was wonderful. She was the greatest support conceivable. She put up with a lot. And did it very cheerfully. And reared four children while all this was going on. A lot of that fell on her.

CARROLL: She must have thought she was married to Woodrow Wilson.

LINK: (Laughs.) Yeah, I think she did.

CARROLL: In a way, you must know more about Woodrow Wilson than an other human being on the face of the earth.

LINK: I think, anyone who reads those volumes, you can know more about Wilson than you can know about any other human being. I don't think that's an exaggeration. You can really follow him, hour by hour, day by day.

CARROLL: And that wasn't everything. So you know even more than that.

LINK: Yeah, that's true. (Laughs.) It's not everything, by any means.

CARROLL: So how do you feel about that, as the big period comes here?

LINK: Well, first of all, you're very glad and very relieved to be relieved of all this burden of work, unrelenting…. It's like laying railroad ties from New York to San Francisco. You don't think you're ever going to get it done. It's discipline getting to the office every morning at eight-thirty and leaving at six. And working weekends. As you get older, your physical energy diminishes and you're very glad to be done with that…. Then there's a feeling of enormous satisfaction, and I might even say pride, when I look at those volumes, that I was able to organize a project and actually finish the project. A large project. And somewhat surprised by that fact, I must say. Because I never expected to finish them.

CARROLL: Really?

LINK: No. And I don't mean this in an invidious way, because there are reasons why these other projects are slow, and some are not slow, some of them are doing very well. But looking at the track record of the other big projects, I expected to work on this about thirty-five years and maybe be about two-thirds of the way, two-thirds finished. So there's a feeling of satisfaction, pride, relief. And yet in a way, I miss it. It gave a structure to my life. It gave me something exciting. Now mind you, there were long periods of tedium, but there were many periods of great excitement. I don't think any historian has ever been given the opportunity to do so much interesting work. Well, [Edward] Gibbon did, for example, over a thirty-year period, and I don't compare myself to Gibbon. But I think what we did and the scholarly way can be compared. He's the great historian of all times.

CARROLL: … Do you think where we are now, in our current knowledge of American presidents, do you think anything – I know this is immodest. I'm trying to solicit an immodest answer to this – but do you think there is any body of work that could possibly measure up to what we have on Wilson? There's a lot of stuff written on Abraham Lincoln and we know half if it is fiction and a lot of baloney.

LINK: The Lincoln papers are quite small....

CARROLL: Although we are finding more now....

LINK: They are finding more. Exactly, right.

CARROLL: But of all the presidents, this is the most documented life we have so far. Maybe when they're done with George Washington.

LINK: Washington, [Thomas] Jefferson, [James] Madison, [Ulysses S.] Grant....

CARROLL: Andrew Jackson ... and Andrew Johnson is being done....

LINK: Andrew Johnson ... what others? That's about it. [James K.] Polk ... and a couple of others.

CARROLL: And curse the people who've burned papers.

LINK: Yeah, that's right.

CARROLL: But the documentation of Wilson's life is the most complete of any president.

LINK: Of any president, yeah.

CARROLL: Will we be able to do this with future presidents? Is this practical? We don't have letter-writers any more. Well, George Bush is a letter-writer. But are presidents of this late era of a different breed and do we run the presidency in such a different way that we would not be able to document, say, Bill Clinton's life, maybe fifty, a hundred years hence?

LINK: I think that's true.

CARROLL: Is it impossible to do?

LINK: Well, we don't know. Maybe. I don't know whether [Clinton] wrote when he was in England, whether he corresponded, we just don't know. We don't know what kind of papers there are from his early life, his early career.

I think we will be able fully to document presidential administrations and, not so much by letters, but mainly by memoranda, reports, and so forth. Whether we're going to be able to do this as we can do with Wilson or Theodore Roosevelt or even as late as Herbert Hoover, say, do this through the papers of the president, is going to be a big question. I doubt that.

It's going to be more documentation for various aspects of an administration's life. For example: Warren Kimball's three-volume edition of the correspondence between Roosevelt and Churchill. Marvelous edition. And I think we probably have to do it that way with Franklin Roosevelt. But unless future presidents are very unusual, I would say beginning with now or even [Jimmy] Carter, we don't know about Carter's personal ... anyway, anyone who was a young person starting in the '70s forward will not have any personal papers because people have stopped writing letters for the most part. It's very rare, indeed. The telephone has absolutely wrecked personal historical documentation.

My wife used to write every one of our children once a week. My mother wrote me every week. I wrote her every week. And then telephone rates came down, and she's written very few letters the last twenty years.

Now I'm not worried at all about the documentation of the history of an administration because you've got tapes ... most telephone calls are taped, many are transcribed. You may have stuff on electronic wires and so on. That's retrievable. And any important document, there are going to be several copies. That's going to be a problem with volume. I think the only thing we can cope with, even an administration like [Ronald] Reagan's – and certainly Reagan was not a great letter-writer, I imagine he hardly wrote letters at all – there were a lot of important policies that went on, foreign policies, and so on....

CARROLL: Should there be a Woodrow Wilson Library? Would that be nice to have?

LINK: Well, in fact, I think we've got one. Our collection is pretty complete. We got together all the Xeroxed copies. That's in Princeton in the manuscript library. We've got 5,000 to 7,000 original Wilson letters ... and ... a lot [of them were published in *The Papers of Woodrow Wilson*]. Princeton has those. But our collection, I don't know, our collection is well over 500,000 to 600,000 documents. It's an enormous collection. We spent 1959 to 1990-91 collecting it. So that's thirty-two years. We were doing research all the time.

I was doing a lot of it myself. Those last volumes I had to put together because, well, we kind of ran out of steam. When we were down in Washington, we said, "Why don't we do all this later? This is in the future. This is concerning the last two years of the administration." So I had to do that myself. I had some great support from the National Historical Publication and Records Commission, the NHPRC.

CARROLL: This was the last how many volumes?

LINK: It would actually be Volumes 62 through 66. Sixty-seven and 68 are pretty much [easily assembled from Woodrow Wilson's personal] papers, in which they carefully cover the retirement years, 1921 to '24. Wilson's secretary kept his diaries very nicely. There they were.

CARROLL: But Volumes 62 to 66, it almost became a one-man effort?

LINK: I had marvelous support down at the archives in the NHPRC.

CARROLL: But your office staff was getting small?

LINK: Yes, it was. Toward the end, why of course people were looking around for other jobs and I was losing staff. And it was down to two of us at the end, really three of us, two and a half, say, something like that.

CARROLL: It must have been frustrating, like a general. You're almost there and all the troops say, "Well, gee, see ya." You still have to get to the end here. But you did it.

LINK: But we did it. Yeah. We did it.

Afterword

Arthur Stanley Link's editing of *Brother Woodrow* would be his last work. He died of lung cancer on March 26, 1998, in Advance, North Carolina. He was seventy-seven years old.

In the several hours of conversation we had, including over cocktails on his porch with his wife, Margaret (who died in 1996), Link never mentioned the fact that at times during the Wilson project, he had to suspend his own participation because of chronic back trouble that led to major surgeries.

That fact came from Arthur Schlesinger, Jr., who like others who knew him were in awe of Link's dedication and single-mindedness of purpose. Schlesinger told me Link was "a moral force in the profession … a man of such evident integrity and decency."

Friend and Wilson biographer August Heckscher said this of Link and his contribution to history: "For any scholar in the future, to have those primary sources to write from is pure gold … He never faltered, he never gave up on the job a single day…. I would visit him and he'd say, 'Augie, you won't believe it. I've got something here. It's absolutely mind-blowing.'… It's surely one of the great acts of scholarship in this century to have carried it through."

George McGovern had the privilege of being Link's first doctoral candidate at Northwestern University. He remembered Professor Link as "tremendously well organized, remarkably disciplined, an intense man."

"He moved me through the Ph.D program as fast as you could get through," the former South Dakota senator recalled. "You couldn't possibly procrastinate on things. There was no dilly-dallying…. You kept moving along." McGovern finished his doctoral dissertation in about a year.

When McGovern resurrected himself to run for president a third time in 1984, Link helped write some of the candidate's speeches. McGovern told me he thought that "they were great speeches, he helped me with themes, good values to sound." Did Link see McGovern as perhaps another Wilson? "I think he did, although he never told me directly," the ex-candidate said.

Link also was a mentor to students. One of them was a young Princeton University man named Bill Bradley.

Somehow, Link found time to teach and, as already mentioned, write articles and other books. He read and reread the classics, was a devoted opera lover, and was active in the Presbyterian church. He served as co-chairman of the Working Group on Disability in United States Presidents (which advised the White House on policies for handling a chief executive's illness or incapacitation), lectured nearly everywhere, won numerous awards, and was given ten honorary degrees.

But Woodrow Wilson was Link's constant companion. It was a labor of love, and a physical one at that: it was a job done with pen in hand and on typewriters. No computers for him. Not a single word of the sixty-nine volumes of *The Papers of Woodrow Wilson* was generated electronically.

As this distinguished, bespectacled gentleman painstakingly worked day after day, year after year, in Princeton University's Firestone Library, he no doubt felt the very presence of his subject. For Link had picked a particular desk from which to captain his project. It had been used decades earlier by a Princeton University president. His name, of course, was Woodrow Wilson.

A Chronology of Woodrow Wilson's Life

December 28, 1856: Thomas Woodrow Wilson is born in Staunton, Virginia, to Rev. Joseph Ruggles Wilson and Janet Woodrow Wilson. "Tommy" is their third child. He has two sisters, Marion, born in 1851, and Annie, born in 1853. A brother, Joseph "Josie" Wilson, is born in 1866.

1858: The Wilson family moves to Augusta, Georgia. He later attends Mr. Derry's Classical School.

Fall, 1870: The Wilson family moves to Columbia, South Carolina.

1873: Wilson enters Davidson College, Davidson, North Carolina, but leaves the following year.

1874: The Wilson family moves to Wilmington, North Carolina, where young Wilson lives for a year.

Fall, 1875: Wilson enters The College of New Jersey (which changes its name to Princeton University in 1896), Princeton, New Jersey. He is elected to *The Princetonian*, and eventually rises to become managing editor.

Class picture, Princeton University, 1879.

June, 1879: Wilson graduates with a bachelor's degree.

August, 1879: *International Review* publishes Wilson's article "Cabinet Government in the United States."

October, 1879: Wilson enters the University of Virginia Law School. He withdraws after a year.

1881: Wilson abandons his first name, under his mother's encouragement, for his middle one, Woodrow.

1882: Wilson is admitted to the Georgia bar. He and Edward I. Renick open a law practice in Atlanta, but Wilson is bored and the business is short-lived.

Fall, 1882: Wilson begins doctoral work at The Johns Hopkins University in Baltimore, Maryland.

June 24, 1885: Wilson marries Ellen Louise Axson, of Savannah, Georgia, at the Independent Presbyterian Church in Savannah.

September 21, 1885: Wilson becomes associate professor of history and political economy at Bryn Mawr College, Bryn Mawr, Pennsylvania.

April 16, 1886: Woodrow and Ellen Wilson's first daughter, Margaret Axson Wilson, is born in Gainesville, Georgia.

June, 1886: Wilson is awarded his Ph.D from Johns Hopkins.

August 28, 1887: Woodrow and Ellen Wilson's second daughter, Jessie Woodrow Wilson, is born in Gainesville, Georgia.

A mustachioed Wilson (second from left, back row) in Johns Hopkins Glee Club, 1884.

April, 1888: Wilson's mother, Janet, dies.

Fall, 1888: Wilson becomes chair of history and political economy at Wesleyan University in Middletown, Connecticut.

October 16, 1889: Woodrow and Ellen Wilson's third daughter, Eleanor Randolph Wilson, is born.

1890: Wilson becomes chair of jurisprudence and politics at Princeton University.

August 1, 1902: Wilson is elected president of Princeton University.

Princeton's president, the first who was not a member of the clergy.

January 21, 1903: Wilson's father, Joseph, dies.

September 15, 1910: Wilson becomes the Democratic Party's nominee for governor of New Jersey.

November 5, 1910: Wilson is elected governor of New Jersey.

July 2, 1912: After forty-six ballots at the Democratic National Convention in Baltimore, Wilson is nominated for president of the United States.

August 7, 1912: Wilson accepts his nomination in a speech delivered at the governor's summer retreat in Seagirt, New Jersey. His opponents are the incumbent Republican president, William Howard Taft, and the former president and now Progressive Party nominee, Theodore Roosevelt.

November 4-5, 1912: Wilson is elected president of the United States, winning 435 electoral votes to Roosevelt's eighty-eight and Taft's eight. Wilson won almost 6.3 million popular votes, compared with 4.1 million for Roosevelt and nearly 3.5 million for Taft.

March 4, 1913: Wilson is inaugurated the twenty-eighth president of the United States.

April 8, 1913: In the first personal appearance by a president before the Congress since John Adams, Wilson addresses a special session, seeking a change in the tariff laws.

New Jersey's progressive governor, 1910.

Gov. Wilson and his family at their summer resort in Seagirt, New Jersey, c. 1911.

(Opposite, top) Front porch politics at Seagirt, 1912.

(Opposite, bottom) Wilson visiting his birthplace, Staunton, Virginia, December 28, 1912.

THE REAL WOODROW WILSON

June 23, 1913: In another speech before the Congress, Wilson proposes creation of the Federal Reserve system, which becomes reality exactly six months later.

October 3, 1913: Wilson signs legislation that creates the first income tax.

November 25, 1913: The Wilsons' second daughter, Jessie, marries Francis B. Sayre in a White House ceremony.

President-elect Wilson and his wife, Ellen, leaving their Princeton home for the inauguration, March 2, 1913.

THE REAL WOODROW WILSON

The president at work in the White House.

April 21, 1914: As diplomatic tensions mount, the United States and Mexico nearly go to war as Wilson orders the seizure of the Customs House in Vera Cruz, Mexico. The United States is trying to prevent Germany from arming the government of Gen. Victoriano Huerta, which the American government does not recognize. An international mediation of the dispute ensues, and Huerta subsequently leaves office.

May 7, 1914: The Wilsons' third daughter, Eleanor, marries William G. McAdoo in a White House ceremony.

August 4, 1914: The Great War, later to be known as World War I, breaks out in Europe. Wilson issues a proclamation declaring the United States a neutral nation.

August 6, 1914: Wilson's wife, Ellen, dies in the White House of Bright's disease, a kidney ailment.

August 19, 1914: Wilson appeals to Americans to be neutral in the war.

September 26, 1914: Congress passes a key part of Wilson's effort to regulate trusts, the Federal Trade Commission Act.

November 23, 1914: American forces withdraw from Vera Cruz.

February 10, 1915: Wilson warns Germany against violating American neutrality on the seas.

May 7, 1915: The British ocean liner *Lusitania* is sunk by a German submarine. Among the 1,198 dead are 124 Americans.

A July 4th oration in front of Independence Hall, Philadelphia.

May 10, 1915: Wilson delivers a speech in Philadelphia declaring that "there is such a thing as a man being too proud to fight."

June 7, 1915: Secretary of State William Jennings Bryan resigns over fears Wilson is nearing war with Germany over the *Lusitania* sinking.

July 29, 1915: Wilson sends United States Marines to Haiti in effort to impose political stability.

Wilson and his bride-to-be, Edith, at the World Series between the Boston Red Sox and the Philadelphia Phillies, October 9, 1915.

October 7, 1915: Wilson announces his engagement to Edith Bolling Galt.

December 18, 1915: Wilson and Edith Bolling Galt marry in a White House ceremony.

February 22, 1916: Wilson proposes mediating a peace in Europe.

March 15, 1916: Wilson sends United States troops into Mexico to pursue Pancho Villa, leader of Mexican guerillas who had made raids in American territory.

May 27, 1916: Wilson proposes a "universal association of nations" in a Washington speech before the League to Enforce Peace.

June 3, 1916: Congress passes the National Defense Act, a modest step toward strengthening United States land and naval forces.

July 16, 1916: The Democratic National Convention in St. Louis renominates Wilson for a second term as president.

July 11, 1916: Wilson signs the Federal Highway Act, legislation providing federal aid to state roads.

August 4, 1916: Wilson signs the treaty under which the Virgin Islands become a United States territory.

September 1, 1916: Wilson signs legislation banning from interstate commerce products made by child labor.

September 3, 1916: An act creating an eight-hour day for railroad workers is signed by Wilson, settling a railroad strike.

November 7, 1916: Wilson is re-elected president, receiving 277 electoral votes to Republican opponent Charles Evan Hughes's 254.

February 3, 1917: Wilson breaks relations with Germany over its resumption of unrestricted submarine warfare.

February 26, 1917: In a speech before Congress, Wilson seeks the authority to arm United States merchant vessels.

March 5, 1917: Wilson is inaugurated president for his second term. He delivers his address in wind and rain at the Capitol.

April 2, 1917: Wilson asks Congress for a declaration of war against Germany.

April 4, 1917: On an 82-6 vote, the Senate adopts the war resolution.

April 6, 1917: The House of Representatives, by a 373-50 vote, adopts the war resolution, and Wilson signs it at the White House.

May 18, 1917: Wilson signs the Selective Service Act, creating the draft. He also announces that the United States will send an expeditionary force to France.

Arrival in Europe, December 13, 1918, riding with President Raymond Poincaré of France.

October 3, 1917: Legislation doubling the income tax and establishing excise taxes is signed by Wilson.

January 4, 1918: Wilson announces that the government is assuming control of the nation's railroads.

January 8, 1918: In an address before a joint session of Congress, Wilson lays out his "Fourteen Points" for establishing peace.

THE REAL WOODROW WILSON

A sign of great expectations: Rue Madeleine in Paris, December 15, 1918.

September 30, 1918: Wilson delivers a speech before the Senate supporting an amendment giving women the right to vote.

November 11, 1918: Wilson announces the signing of the Armistice, ending the war.

December 4, 1918: Wilson sails for Europe to participate in the Paris Peace Conference.

December 14, 1918: Wilson and his wife, Edith, arrive in Paris.

At headquarters with Gen. John J. Pershing, December 25, 1918.

Crowds in Paris, December 19, 1918.

Flowers along Wilson's way, Dover, England, December 27, 1918.

January 18, 1919: Wilson speaks at the opening session of the peace conference.

January 29, 1919: The Eighteenth Amendment, banning the making, sale, and transport of alcoholic beverages, is ratified, beginning what would become known as Prohibition.

February 14, 1919: Wilson presents a plan for a League of Nations to the peace conference.

March 14, 1919: After about three weeks at home, Wilson returns to Paris for the resumption of the peace conference.

1657907

June 28, 1919: Wilson signs the peace treaty with Germany.

July 8, 1919: Wilson arrives back in the United States, at Hoboken, New Jersey.

July 10, 1919: Wilson presents the plan for a League of Nations to the Senate.

September 3-25, 1919: In an effort to build public support for the League of Nations, Wilson tours the nation by train, making speeches from coast to coast.

Bidding farewell to Europe, June 1919.

September 25-26, 1919: Wilson suffers a transient ischemic attack traveling between Colorado and Kansas. The president's tour is prematurely ended and he returns to Washington.

THE REAL WOODROW WILSON

Campaign for the League: on the western trip, San Francisco, September 1919.

At the microphones, Berkeley, California, September 1919.

October 2, 1919: Wilson suffers a stroke, but that fact and his actual condition are not made public.

November 19, 1919: The Senate rejects the Versailles Treaty.

March 19, 1920: The Senate again rejects the peace treaty.

June 8, 1920: The Republican National Convention in Chicago nominates Warren G. Harding for president and Calvin Coolidge for vice president.

Whistlestop handshake, with the vigilant Adm. Grayson (far left) and Edith in the background, 1919.

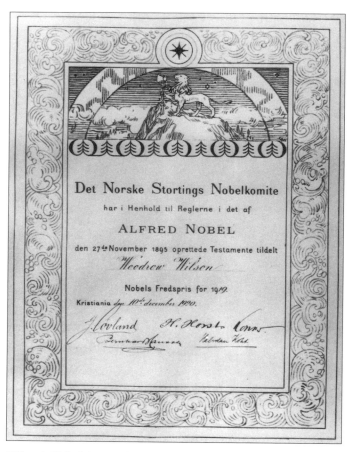

Wilson's Nobel Peace Prize, awarded December 10, 1920. He was unable to receive it in person.

THE REAL WOODROW WILSON

June 28, 1920: Meeting in San Francisco, the Democratic National Convention nominates James M. Cox for president and Franklin D. Roosevelt for vice president.

August 26, 1920: The Nineteenth Amendment, giving women the right to vote, is ratified.

November 2, 1920: Harding is elected president.

November 15, 1920: The League of Nations holds its first meeting in Geneva.

December 10, 1920: Wilson receives the Nobel Peace Prize.

March 4, 1921: Wilson rides with President-elect Harding to the Capitol for the Ohioan's inauguration. Because of his illness, he does not attend the actual ceremonies. He and Mrs. Wilson take up residence at 2340 S Street N.W., in Washington.

November 11, 1921: Wilson briefly rides in part of the funeral procession for an unknown soldier from the war.

Late 1922: The Woodrow Wilson Foundation, set up to perpetuate the former president's ideals, announces it has reached its goal of raising $1 million and begins operations.

The Wilsons at the S Street house in Washington, Armistice Day, November 11, 1922.

August 8, 1923: Wilson accompanies the body of Harding, who has died suddenly in San Francisco, from the White House to the Capitol.

November 10, 1923: Speaking over the radio, Wilson speaks on the significance of Armistice Day. It is his last national address.

November 11, 1923: He speaks to a crowd outside his home: "I am not one of those who have the least anxiety about the triumph of the principles I have stood for."

January 31, 1924: Wilson becomes gravely ill.

February 3, 1924: Lying in his bed at his S Street home, Wilson dies. People waiting outside the house for news kneel in the street and pray at the announcement of his death.

February 6, 1924: Wilson is buried at Washington National Cathedral.

Bibliography

To collect all the books written by and about Woodrow Wilson would take several years and a lot of space. I know, because I have been doing it as part of a larger library on all of the presidents. But do not despair. I have pared down the list to a slightly more manageable size. For the general reader, or for the scholar, the following provides a solid grounding in Woodrow Wilson.

Not as prolific as Theodore Roosevelt, Wilson nevertheless turned out a considerable body of published work: *Congressional Government: A Study in American Politics* (Boston: Houghton, Mifflin and Co., 1885); *The State: Elements of Historical and Practical Politics – A Sketch of Institutional History and Administration* (Boston: D.C. Heath & Co., 1889), and a condensation of part of the larger work, *The State and Federal Governments of the United States: A Brief Manual for Schools and Colleges* (Boston: D.C. Heath & Co., 1889); *Division and Reunion, 1829-1889* (New York and London: Longmans, Green and Co., 1893); *An Old Master and Other Political Essays* (New York: Charles Scribner's Sons, 1893); *Mere Literature and Other Essays* (Boston: Houghton, Mifflin and Co., 1896); *George Washington* (New York and London: Harper & Brothers, 1897); *A History of the American People* (New York and London: Harper & Brothers, 1902); *Consti-*

tutional Government in the United States (New York: The Columbia University Press, 1908); *The Free Life* (New York: Thomas Y. Crowell & Co., 1908); *The Minister and the Community* (New York and London: Association Press, 1912); *The New Freedom: A Call for the Emancipation of the Generous Energies of a People* (New York: Doubleday, Page & Co., 1913); *The Road Away from Revolution* (Boston: The Atlantic Monthly Press, 1923); and *Robert E. Lee* (Chapel Hill: The University of North Carolina Press, 1924).

Wilson's election as president prompted Harper and Brothers Publishers in New York to bring out some separate small volumes of Wilson's writings and speeches: *When a Man Comes to Himself* (1915); *On Being Human* (1916); *The President of the United States* (1916); *In Our First Year of War* (1917); *Why We Are At War* (1917); *Guarantees of Peace* (1919); *International Ideals* (1919); *The Triumph of Ideals* (1919); *The Hope of the World* (1920).

And, it goes without saying, since we've already rather covered the matter, that *The Papers of Woodrow Wilson* (Princeton, N.J.: Princeton University Press, 1966-1994), edited by Arthur S. Link in all their sixty-nine volume glory and heft, are the *sine qua non* for research on the twenty-eighth president.

Link and Wilson enthusiasts also will want to consult these books by the former about the latter: *The Higher Realism of Woodrow Wilson and Other Essays*

(Nashville: Vanderbilt University Press, 1971); *Wilson the Diplomatist: A Look at His Major Foreign Policies* (Baltimore: The Johns Hopkins Press, 1957); *Wilson: The Road to the White House* (Princeton, N.J.: Princeton University Press, 1947); *Wilson: The New Freedom* (Princeton, N.J.: Princeton University Press, 1956); *Wilson: The Struggle for Neutrality, 1914-1915* (Princeton, N.J.: Princeton University Press, 1960); *Wilson: Confusion and Crises, 1915-1916* (Princeton, N.J.: Princeton University Press, 1964); *Wilson: Campaigns for Progressivism and Peace, 1916-1917* (Princeton, N.J.: Princeton University Press, 1965); *Woodrow Wilson: A Brief Biography* (Cleveland: The World Publishing Co., 1963); *Woodrow Wilson and a Revolutionary World, 1913-1921* (Chapel Hill: University of North Carolina Press, 1982); *Woodrow Wilson and the Progressive Era, 1910-1917* (New York: Harper & Brothers, Publishers, 1954); *Woodrow Wilson: A Profile* (New York: Hill & Wang, 1968); and *Woodrow Wilson: Revolution, War, and Peace* (Arlington Heights, Ill.: Harlan Davidson, Inc., 1979).

The most complete, and certainly daunting, early work on Wilson is, as Link discussed, by Ray Stannard Baker. It was published in eight volumes under the title *Woodrow Wilson: Life and Letters* (Garden City, N.Y.: Doubleday, Page & Co., and Doubleday, Doran & Co., 1927-1939).

For a single-volume, complete modern work on Wilson, August Heckscher's *Woodrow Wilson: A Biography* (New York: Charles Scribner's Sons, 1991) is unsurpassed, drawing as it does on the Wilson papers Link had assembled.

A by no means complete list of other useful Wilson works includes: *"Brother Woodrow": A Memoir of Woodrow Wilson,* Stockton Axson (Princeton, N.J.: Princeton University Press, 1993); *Woodrow Wilson and the Politics of Morality,* John Morton Blum (Boston: Little, Brown and Co., 1956); *The Presidency of Woodrow Wilson,* Kendrick A. Clements (Lawrence: University Press of Kansas, 1992); *The Wilson Era: Essays in Honor of Arthur S. Link,* John Milton Cooper and Charles E. Neu (Arlington Heights, Ill.: Harlan Davidson, Inc., 1991); *The Warrior and the Priest: Woodrow Wilson and Theodore Roosevelt,* John Milton Cooper (Cambridge, Mass.: The Belknap Press of Harvard University Press, 1983); *The Wilson Era: Years of Peace,* 1910-1917, Josephus Daniels (Chapel Hill: University of North Carolina Press, 1944); *The Wilson Era: Years of War and After, 1917-1923,* Josephus Daniels (Chapel Hill: University of North Carolina Press, 1946); *Woodrow Wilson: An Intimate Memoir,* Cary T. Grayson (New York: Holt, Rinehart and Winston, 1960); *The Ordeal of Woodrow Wilson,* Herbert Hoover (New York: McGraw-Hill Book Co., Inc., 1958); *To End All Wars:*

Woodrow Wilson and the Quest for a New World Order, Thomas J. Knock (New York and London: Oxford University Press, 1992); *The Woodrow Wilsons,* Eleanor Wilson McAdoo (New York: The Macmillan Co., 1937); *Woodrow Wilson: A Life for World Peace,* Jan Willem Schulte Nordholdt (Berkeley: University of California Press, 1991); *The Intimate Papers of Colonel House,* Charles Seymour, editor (Boston: Houghton Mifflin Co., 4 volumes, 1926-1928); *Woodrow Wilson as I Know Him,* Joseph P. Tumulty (Garden City, N.Y.: Doubleday, Page & Co., 1921).

The most formidable catalogue of works on the twenty-eighth president is *Woodrow Wilson: A Bibliography,* John M. Mulder, Ernest M. White, and Ethel S. White, editors (Westport, Conn., and London: Greenwood Press, 1997).

THE REAL WOODROW WILSON

Sources of Illustrations

With the exception of those listed below, all illustrations are courtesy of the Woodrow Wilson House – a National Trust Historic Site, Washington, DC. (Page 87 photograph is by Pach Brothers)

Back cover and page 62: portrait of Arthur S. Link, courtesy of the photographer, Seny Norasingh.

Cover portrait of the author, and Wilson trunks on page 12: courtesy of the photographer, Bill Perry.

xxiv: portrait of Arthur S. Link in the 1960s, courtesy of the Link family.

30: pastel portrait of Woodrow Wilson by Fred Yates, England, 1906, courtesy of the Woodrow Wilson Birthplace Foundation, Staunton, Virginia.

85: Glee Club photograph, Ferdinand Hamburger, Jr. Archives of The Johns Hopkins University.

88: Woodrow Wilson family by Rudolph Eickemeyer, Jr., Photographic History Collection, National Museum of American History, Smithsonian Institution, negative number 85-8660.

IMAGES FROM THE PAST

Publishing history in ways that help people see it for themselves

WHITE FIRE

Stuart Murray

In 1828, frontiersman Dirk Arendt is guiding an archaeological expedition toward a lost city near Zululand when he learns that the leader of his party is an agent of a ruthless secret brotherhood. This agent is on a mission to find an ancient amulet said to be in the hands of Shaka, founder and lord of the Zulu nation. The amulet and its central Stone of White Fire — so named because it radiates a hypnotizing white glow — has the power to reveal King Solomon's fabled diamond fields and gold mines. More than that, say the legends, the amulet can bring great wisdom if used in the right way. If misused, it dooms its bearer to a life of torment. Dirk's expedition arrives in Zululand just as rebels are about to overthrow Shaka. The rebels, too, desire to possess the Amulet of White Fire as a token of Shaka's magic power.

Meanwhile, far to the southwest, the first Cape Colony pioneers (voortrekkers) journey northward into the wilderness in search of the Promised Land. These independent-minded folk include Dirk's own parents and an idealistic young woman, Rachel Drente. The trekkers do not yet know it, but the land they intend to settle on is rich in diamonds and gold just beneath its surface. The very wealth sought after by the secret brotherhood. Dirk and Rachel fall in love, but there seems little hope when they are caught between Zulu regiments and the conspirators who are seeking the Amulet of White Fire.

5.5" x 8.5", 325 pages ISBN 1-884592-25-2 Hardcover $26.00

WASHINGTON'S FAREWELL TO HIS OFFICERS:
After Victory in the Revolution
Stuart Murray

In the sunlit Long Room of Fraunces Tavern, on a winter's day in New York City, 1783, George Washington's few remaining officers anxiously await his arrival. He has called them here to say goodbye—likely never to see them again. The British redcoats have sailed away, defeated in the Revolution. This moving incident, one almost forgotten in American history, was among the most telling and symbolic events of the War for Independence.

As they anticipate their beloved general's arrival, the officers recall how their struggle for the sacred cause flickered, almost went out, then flared into final victory. In the story of Washington's Farewell are the memories of long-struggling patriots—the famous and the little-known—men committed heart and soul to the cause of American liberty: Knox, McDougall, Lamb, Hamilton, Steuben, Shaw, Humphreys, Varick, Burnett, Hull, Fish, Tallmadge, the Clintons, Van Cortlandt, Fraunces… Heroes all. Index. Bibliography. 42 prints and maps.

5" x 7", 240 pages ISBN 1-884592-20-1 Hardcover $21.00

AMERICA'S SONG: The Story of Yankee Doodle
Stuart Murray

During the first uncertain hours of the Revolution, British redcoats sang "Yankee Doodle" as an insult to Americans—but when the rebels won astounding victories this song of insult was transformed to a song of triumph, eventually becoming "America's Song."

This is the first complete chronicle of the story of "Yankee Doodle," perhaps the best-known tune in all the world. From its early days an ancient air for dancing, through the era of Dutch and Puritan colonial settlement, "Yankee Doodle" evolved during the French and Indian Wars and the American Revolution to become our most stirring anthem of liberty. Index. Bibliography. Illustrated with 37 prints and maps.

5" x 7", 248 pages ISBN 1-884592-18-X Hardcover $21.00

RUDYARD KIPLING IN VERMONT: Birthplace of The Jungle Books
Stuart Murray

This book fills a gap in the biographical coverage of the important British author who is generally described as having lived only in India and England. It provides the missing links in the bitter-sweet story that haunts the portals of Naulakha, the distinctive shingle style home built by Kipling and his American wife near Brattleboro, Vermont. Here the Kiplings lived for four years and the first two of their three children were born.

All but one of Kipling's major works stem from these years of rising success, happiness and productivity; but because of a feud with his American brother-in-law, Beatty, which was seized on by newspaper reporters eager to put a British celebrity in his place, the author and his family left their home in America forever in 1896.

6" x 9"; 208 pages; Extensive index. Excerpts from Kipling poems, 21 historical photos; 6 book illustrations; and 7 sketches convey the mood of the times, character of the people, and style of Kipling's work.

ISBN 1-884592-04-X Hardcover $29.00
ISBN 1-884592-05-8 Paperback $18.95

THE HONOR OF COMMAND: Gen. Burgoyne's Saratoga Campaign
Stuart Murray

Leaving Quebec in June, Burgoyne was confident in his ability to strike a decisive blow against the rebellion in the colonies. Instead, the stubborn rebels fought back, slowed his advance and inflicted irreplaceable losses, leading to his defeat and surrender at Saratoga on October 17, 1777 — an important turning point in the American Revolution. Burgoyne's point of view as the campaign progresses is expressed from his dispatches, addresses to his army, and exchanges with friends and fellow officers. ; 33 prints and engravings, 8 maps, 10 sketches. Index

7" x 10", 128 pages ISBN 1-884592-03-1 Paperback $14.95

NORMAN ROCKWELL AT HOME IN VERMONT:
The Arlington Years, 1939-1953
Stuart Murray

Norman Rockwell painted some of his greatest works, including "The Four Freedoms" during the 15 years he and his family lived in Arlington, Vermont. Compared to his former home in the suburbs of New York City, it was "like living in another world," and completely transformed his already successful career as America's leading illustrator. For the first time he began to paint pictures that "grew out of the every day life of my neighbors."

32 historical photographs, 13 Rockwell paintings and sketches, and personal recollections. Index. Regional map, selected bibliography, and listing of area museums and exhibitions.

7" x 10", 96 pages ISBN 1-884592-02-3 Paperback $14.95

THE ESSENTIAL GEORGE WASHINGTON:
Two Hundred Years of Observations on the Man, Myth and Patriot
Peter Hannaford

Why did Thomas Paine turn against him? Why did Elizabeth Powel call him "impudent"? What is the truth about the cherry tree story? What was his single most important quality? These and many more questions about the man called "the father of his country" are answered in this collection. The reader meets Washington's contemporaries, followed by famous Americans from the many decades between then and now and, finally, well-known modern-day Americans. Included are Benjamin Franklin, Thomas Jefferson, Abigail Adams, Parson Weems, Abraham Lincoln, Walt Whitman, Woodrow Wilson, Bob Dole, George McGovern, Eugene McCarthy, Letitia Baldrige, Newt Gingrich, Ronald Reagan—and many more. Read in small doses or straight through—either way, the book gives a full portrait of the man who—more than any other—made the United States of America possible. Over 60 prints and photographs.

5" x 7", 190 pages ISBN 1-884592-23-6 Hardcover $19.50

LETTERS TO VERMONT Volumes I and II:
From Her Civil War Soldier Correspondents to the Home Press
Donald Wickman, Editor/Compiler

In their letters "To the Editor" of the Rutland Herald, young Vermont soldiers tell of fighting for the Union, galloping around Lee's army in Virginia, garrisoning the beleaguered defenses of Washington, D.C., and blunting Pickett's desperate charge at Gettysburg. One writer is captured, another serves as a prison camp guard, others are wounded — and one dies fighting in the horrific conflict in the Wilderness of Virginia. Biographical information for each writer (except one who remains an enigma) and supporting commentary on military affairs. 54 engravings and prints, 32 contemporary maps, 45 historical photographs. Extensive index.

Vol. 1, 6" x 9", 251 pages ISBN 1-884592-10-4 Hardcover $30.00
ISBN 1-884592-11-2 Paper $19.95

Vol. 2, 6" x 9", 265 pages ISBN 1-884592-16-3 Hardcover $30.00
ISBN 1-884592-17-1 Paper $19.95

ALLIGATORS ALWAYS DRESS FOR DINNER:
An Alphabet Book of Vintage Photographs
Linda Donigan and Michael Horwitz

A collection of late 19th- and early 20th-century images from around the world reproduced in rich duo tone for children and all who love historical pictures. Each two-page spread offers a surprising visual treat: Beholding Beauty - a beautifully dressed and adorned Kikuyu couple; Fluted Fingers - a wandering Japanese Zen monk playing a bamboo recorder; and Working the Bandwagon - the Cole Brothers Band on an elaborate 1879 circus wagon. A-Z information pages with image details.

9 1/4" x 9 3/4", 64 pages ISBN 1-884592-08-2 Hardcover $25.00

REMEMBERING GRANDMA MOSES
Beth Moses Hickok

Grandma Moses, a crusty, feisty, upstate New York farm wife and grand-mother, as remembered in affectionate detail by Beth Moses Hickok, who married into the family at 22, and raised two of Grandma's grand-daughters. Set in 1934, before the artist was "discovered", the book includes family snapshots, and photographs that evoke the landscape of Eagle Bridge, home for most of her century-plus life. Two portraits of Grandma Moses - a 1947 painting and a 1949 photograph, and nine historical photographs. On the cover is a rare colorful yarn painting given to the author as a wedding present.

6" x 9", 64 pages ISBN 1-884592-01-5 Paperback $12.95

REMAINS UNKNOWN
Michael J. Caduto
with sixteen pencil sketches by Adelaide Murphy Tyrol

He somehow found his way to Vermont soon after the Mexican War. It was a long journey, the beginning of a private purgatory that lasted over 150 years. At last, with the help of friends he'd never met, he took the final steps in a quiet cemetery by the river on a sultry afternoon.

In this strange and haunting tale, based on a true story, the reader enters a world suspended between our earthly existence and the realm of the human spirit. A small community of people embarks on an adventure that compels them to bring the mysterious, mummified remains of one long dead to a resting place of peace and grace. With help from two distinct spiritual traditions, and a dose of healing humor in the face of grief, the journey unfolds with a sense of dignity and compassion.

5" x 7", 80 pages ISBN 1-884592-24-4 Hardcover $15.00

Available at your local bookstore or from
Images from the Past, Inc.,
888-442-3204 for credit card orders;
PO Box 137, Bennington, VT 05201 with check or money order.

When ordering, please add $4.00 shipping and handling
for the first book and $1 for each additional.

(Add 5% sales tax for shipments to Vermont.)

www.ImagesfromthePast.com